Gorillas in the Myth
A Duck Soup Reader

revisited and revised a smidgeon
by Cecil Bothwell

Brave Ulysses Books
2008

Gorillas in the Myth: A Duck Soup Reader
Second Edition
ISBN:978-0-6151-8969-7
Brave Ulysses Books
POB 1877
Asheville, NC 28802

Gorillas in the Myth

To Jeanne

Also by the author:
The Icarus Glitch: Another Duck Soup Reader (2001)
Finding Your Way in Asheville (2005)
(with Betsy Ball and Steve Shanafelt)
The Prince of War: Billy Graham's Crusade for a Wholly Christian Empire (2007)

Index

Introduction   9
I. Bring it on home
    Ancestral voices   16
    The white paper white paper   19
    Quitcher bitchin   22
    The current buzz   25
    Costing cookies   28
    Exploding intentions   31
    Working mischief, working wonders   34
    Woo-woo versus the bunny-hug   37

II. It's breakin' my heart in two
    Look both ways   42
    Dark enough to see   45
    Whirl away   48
    On a wing and a prayer   51
    Trapped   54
    Seeing trees in the forest   57
    Scaling hope   60

III. Until you use me up
    Stone tablets and all that   64
    Dinosaur juice   67
    Water fights   70
    The horse's mouth   73
    Good things from the garden   76
    Where ignorant armies clash by night   79
    High hopes in Glen Canyon   82

IV. The way you do the things you do

The rules are not different here 86

How you gonna keep 'em down in Belize? 89

Let it rain 92

The crystal plummets 95

Sprawl: urban and other 98

Goin' down to Yasgur's farm 101

All I need is the air that I breathe 104

Winnowing, winnowing 107

The killing fields 110

The change is gonna do me good 113

V. Not the economy, stupid

Live complexly that others may ... 117

One, two, three, four, look at the score 120

How do like them apples? 123

Remember, buy here now 126

Jobs? or work? 129

Dick's and Jane's addictions 132

Gorillas in the myth 135

Acknowledgements 138

Introduction

Goldilocks had it all figured out: Not too cold, not too hot—just right! It works for soup and it works for planets, too. While some might argue that on a different world we would simply be different, the evidence suggests that if the world was only a little less "just right" we wouldn't be here at all. Water is an essential ingredient for life, and the water needs to be liquid to make the sort of primordial soup in which life can get going. If the earth were slightly further from the sun, the soup would be frozen. If the earth were slightly closer it would have boiled dry—and all the other ingredients would be stuck to the bottom of the pan.

As it is, life did emerge and—during four billion years of tinkering—it managed to produce our lovely biosphere. Starting with noxious air and a global ocean full of dissolved poisons, living cells have worked to make it just right. Toxins have been locked up through sequestration and sedimentation—mostly tucked out of harm's way beneath the earth's crust. Meanwhile plants and animals learned to recycle each other's less toxic wastes to the benefit of all.

Ain't it sweet?

Sadly, this beautiful planet is under siege.

Globe-girdling corporations—the mythical gorillas in my title essay—have created a new colonialism. They extract resources without regard for local need or biospheric impact; build and continually relocate production facilities where labor or resources are cheap, and export their wares to high-dollar markets; manipulate demand with dominance of information media; use their economic muscle to command special treatment including tax relief and infrastructure subsidies from local governments; and impoverish the great majority while concentrating money and power in the hands of a few. These corporations are utterly dependent on under-priced petroleum and electric power. And this meta-colonialism is far more powerful than that of an earlier era, because the big players have now escaped the cages of nationalistic homelands and are busy writing our new international-trade laws. The World Bank, the International Monetary Fund, and the World Trade Organization are the enforcers who whip peasants and bureaucrats into compliance.

If wells were bottomless, forests unlimited, oceans unbounded and the biosphere deep and wide enough to absorb unending waste, the greed and rapaciousness of meta-colonialists might be tolerable. Unfortunately there are limits.

Our current technological civilization is on a collision course with physical realities which we cannot change. Human numbers will soon top out at 8 to 10 billion; arable acreage is diminishing; food stocks are at a modern historic per-capita low; fisheries are collapsing; many major mineral resources will run out in the next century; forests worldwide are in steep decline; an extinction spasm is wracking the earth's diversity of life forms; and the planet is warming. Most troubling of all, our industrial methods are releasing poisons locked out of the biosphere for millenia, and introducing new ones: we are re-toxifying the soup of life. I don't make this stuff up, and imagining that they are not critical problems will not make them go away.

Technoptimists among us believe we can and will simply invent our way out of our fix. "Humans are clever," runs this argument, "We were born of adversity when retreating woodlands forced us out of the trees and into the savannah. We were forged amidst glacial ice flows. We harnessed plants and animals and chemical compounds to do our bidding. We have unwound the spiral helices of DNA and are reinventing species to suit our whims. We have peered into the depths of atoms and into the vast reaches of space. We have triumphed!"

"Well, sort of," I hasten to interject.
"And at great cost."

The last time we Westerners were really crowded and faced an abrupt climate change about half of us died of the Black Plague. On the upside, survivors of that little hiccup enjoyed higher wages, lower housing costs and an agricultural surplus as the weather improved. If that's your idea of success, however, please don't include me in your plans. When the Chinese confronted a similar scenario in an earlier era, peasants sold or traded their children as food, being understandably reluctant to eat their own. (So much for the joy of cooking.) Triumph has its costs.

Ah, but we have already applied the brakes, have we not? The birth rate is falling faster than anyone expected a decade ago. Recycling and energy efficiency are trans-forming industry. Hybrid vehicles and fuel cells are poised to reinvent transportation. The Human Genome Project! The cell phone! The Internet!

Yes. And AIDS may do for (and to) Africa and Asia what the Bubonic Plague did for Europe.

Notwithstanding the looming disaster, though, I remain hopeful. Massive shifts of consciousness can occur: Witness the Soviet collapse, or the Copernican revolution that toppled geocentrism. We can make the leap from a linear, extractive, poisonous society to a circular, regenerative and benign existence. The essays collected here reflect not only my efforts to discard myths which could prove to be life-threatening, but also the joy I find exploring the natural world. There is much worth saving on our miraculous planetary home.

New inventions will unquestionably play a huge part in a successful transition to a sustainable culture, but it is the changes that we can adopt today that will buy us time to discover miracle cures. We can pull back from consumerism—and from producing more consumers. We can divert our dollars toward the most efficient vehicles on the market—and drive less. We can inhabit smaller homes that are well insulated and ventilated—and reject the trend toward climate controlled show-homes with automatic everything. We can choose organic food—and give farmers the incentive they need to shift. We can invest in environmentally sensitive regional companies— and demand change from others whose stock we own. One decision at a time, we can work together to fashion a culture which might endure.

Perhaps more than anything else we need to re-think our mythology and consider different icons for our mental pedestals. We have embraced economic growth as an end in itself, without asking whether that growth can create an enduringly livable world. In the past century or so we have substituted an imaginary ledger for the natural accounting system which evolved over billions of years. We have cooked the books, to the point that we can no longer differentiate meaningful gain from life destroying deficit—as when a clear-cut rainforest is tabulated as profit while investment in photovoltaic panels creates a loss.

Maybe we need to redefine what winning means if that which we usually label "winning" inherently causes irremediable harm. So herewith—embracing high hope for the survival of gorillas, gazelles, galapagos tortoises, whales, wildebeests, wolves, rhinos, echinas and mynnhas (not to mention Mama Bear, Papa Bear, Baby Bear and our putatively sapient selves)—some Soup.

•••

It is eight years since I wrote the foregoing introduction and there isn't much I would change today, except to note that climate change appears to be moving faster than most of us imagined at the turn of the century. And, of course, we have endured almost eight years of rule by a sociopathic fool who has delayed meaningful change while waging his holy war. Reading ahead, I see that there isn't much I would alter in the original essays, either. But I've made a few notes where appropriate. If we don't change our minds once in a while, we can't make much claim to be learning as we go along.

Note: *Earlier versions of the following material originally appeared in my syndicated column,* Duck Soup: Essays on the Submerging Culture. *Various among them have been published in* The Dayton Voice, Brandywine Valley Advocate, Catalyst, CityBeat, Colorado Springs Independent, Mountain Living Magazine, Mountain Xpress, Orlando Weekly, Rapid River, *and South Carolina's journal of conscience,* Point. *Many were aired during a three year run on WNCW 88.7 FM in Spindale, North Carolina. All were published in my weekly* Soupletter, *between 1993 and 1999.*

It was a blog in the days before there were blogs. Now I blog at:

http://bothwellsblog.wordpress.com

I. Bring it on home

Ah yes, you say, but what about Mozart? Punk rock? Astrophysics? Flush toilets? Potato chips? Silicon chips? Oral surgery? The Super Bowl and the World Series? Our coming journey to the stars? Vital projects, I agree, and I support them all. (On a voluntary basis only.) But why not a compromise? Why not—both? Why can't we have a moderate number of small cities, bright islands of electricity and kultur and industry surrounded by shoals of farmland, cow range, and timberland, set in the midst of a great unbounded sea of primitive forest, unbroken mountains, virgin desert? The human reason can conceive of such a free and spacious world; why can't we allow it to become—again —our home?

The American Indians had no word for what we call "wilderness." For them the wilderness was home.

~**Edward Abbey**
Down the River

Ancestral voices

Walking a wilderness beach on the Gulf of Mexico, I looked at sea shells—hearing my mother's voice. "Moon shell," she said, pointing at a beautifully polished globular spiral snail. "Sand dollar," she announced, holding a delicate flat disk with a flower etched on its center. Then "Angel wing, sea urchin, lace murex and olive shell" echoed in my mind.

There were whispers of my grandmother's voice, too, as my memory stretched back nearly 40 years, to another walk on another beach: Sanibel Island, with its crunchy sugar sand, and a ferry-boat ride where I watched manta rays and dolphins slide through crystal-green water.

"Sand dollar," I repeated as I picked one up, intact, and brushed sand from the pattern.

The timelessness of that experience struck echoes, traces of an oral tradition stretching back beyond history: the primal gatherer/hunter educational system that predates language. Once, there were apes who taught their young what was good to eat and what was poisonous by example. Perhaps there were grunts of approval; later, there were words.

"Clam. Snail. Edible. Toxic."

Hearing my mother's voice, some deep chord of order and belonging seemed to resonate. True, she was teaching me the names of things prized for their beauty, not for their use as food; but the process was the same. And, of course, even ornament boasts a venerable heritage. A Native American mother would have pointed out the quahog clam to her curious child, treasured not just for food, but also for the purple shell that would be cut and drilled for wampum beads.

Mother to child, the vital cultural information still flows. "Levi, Lee, Calvin Klein, Jordache," sounds the shopping-mall litany. "Folger's, Chock Full o' Nuts, Taster's Choice," declaims the grocery-store cadence. And even if the commercial façade of a shopping venue lacks the immemorial grace of a deserted beach buffeted by salt wind and the crying of gulls, the function is the same. Another generation on, a middle-aged man will hear whispers of maternal guidance as he picks a pair of pants.

The urge to provide for ourselves, to forage for what sustains us, is as natural as breathing. If the wilderness search for edible berries and mushrooms has segued into hastily piling microwave dinners and boxes of pasta in a shopping cart, it is because the wilderness itself has been supplanted by pavement. Our needs remain, and the words "home cooked" retain a power not entirely erased by commercial exploitation. Home cooked is what mother fed us, saying: "Eat your peas. Peas are good for you."

I have heard it said that shopping malls are popular because they're a safe place to act out our gatherer/hunter instincts. Perhaps that is part of the comfort many folks find in excursions there. More than once, I have heard people say they shop when they are depressed, and it cheers them. It must be those ancient echoes of a time when successful gathering meant survival, when looking and picking up and evaluating were the most crucial acts in a day.

Next time you're at the beach, watch the people moving along the strand. They stoop and examine and exclaim. They scan the horizon, briefly, then look down again. A scrap of sand-polished, broken glass, or a bit of driftwood, catches the imagination. "This looks like a ruby! This looks like a running deer!" Pictures from a cave-wall exhibition. Shadows in the firelight.

We are so much composed of what we have been, so much the result of history and genes, it is difficult to pick out the threads that make the cloth from which we're cut. The powerful emotion that swept me on that wilderness beach was a moment of discovery: the naming of names, the singing of my mother and my more distant ancestors, the chords of life that tie us, one to another, in an ancient dance. "Moon shell, sand dollar, angel wing"—I hear the voices of the ages, and I understand. The tapestry is seamless; I am in and of the Earth.

The white-paper White Paper

A couple of months ago, while listening to a public-radio program called *Marketplace*, I heard an unattributed statistic that has bugged me ever since.

The topic was toilet tissue. A reporter asserted that the average American uses one roll of this product per week, meaning fifty-two rolls per year. This, we were told, translates into whole forests being flushed. Finally, it was asserted that (unnamed) environmental groups advocate the use of bidets instead of t.p. as a conservation move.

Hmmm.

Taken at face value, that story seems fair enough. But should we accept any of it uncritically? As reporters on *Marketplace* are fond of quipping, "Let's do the numbers."

I have spent the summer counting little white squares; I find that I use eight sheets per day, sometimes ten. Plotted over an eight-week period, the average is 8.45 per diem. My product of choice claims to offer one thousand sheets per roll (I have not corroborated this, but it seems plausible, based on my replacement rate). A little fancy arithmetic reveals that I use about three rolls per year—a far cry from fifty-two.

In round numbers, that is a 2,000 percent error. Not trivial.

Clearly, there are physiological differences between the sexes—easily noted in public restrooms, where there are never paper dispensers above urinals— that suggest a higher rate of use by women. And doubtless, many men are neither as neat nor as parsimonious as I, in the matter at hand. Still, if I triple male use and accept the roll-per-week figure for females, I arrive at a guesstimate of 30 per year. Again, not a trivial discrepancy.

Now to the second part of the story: bidets. I have seen exactly one of these little marvels in my life and have never availed myself of their graces. I presume they function as advertised, but must confess this is an untested axiom. It appears obvious that, if a bidet does what it claims, it will leave a portion of one's anatomy wet.

Air drying is a possibility I deem unlikely for a nation in a hurry. Surely—in public places, at least—the need for absorption will be met with paper. I would be wildly surprised if the standard answer in bidet-equipped homes proved markedly different. Unless there is a sea change in the personal-care-products industry, I cannot fathom what an average consumer would use for this purpose, other than toilet tissue.

I also surmise that a bidet leaves one's nether portion wetter than urination. (Do women, in fact, use bidets after urination? Bear with me, if this whole discussion seems to be tending toward the indelicate.) From my infrequent use of paper towels on kitchen surfaces, I can attest that a wetter counter demands more absorption. This suggests that those who avail themselves of European plumbing may very well use more paper, not less.

Experimenting with my own eight squares, I find that they do not soak up much liquid, and I would be greatly amazed if using a bidet reduced my paper use by so much as a jot.

Summing up my little thought experiment, I remain unconvinced that bidets significantly impact toilet-paper use.

All that would be only so much blather, were it not for the source. *Marketplace* purports to be an accurate provenance for economic numbers. Of what possible use is a financial story that's 2,000 percent off base? Are all of their statistics equally unreliable? Or are they secretly funded by a consortium of bidet vendors seeking to flood the American market?

And, speaking for one (named) environmentalist—myself—the real problem isn't toilet paper, it's our plumbing. My composting toilet system has plausibly saved more than 300,000 gallons of water—and an immeasurable volume of organic water pollution—over the past twenty years. On a larger scale, mixing household and industrial wastes in our sewage systems creates a chemical soup that causes nothing but trouble. But that's another story—with other numbers and other answers—for another day.

Quitcher bitchin

My people were dispossessed of their ancestral land, evicted from the dirt that had fed them for generations, driven from the ground where my forebears are buried. They were shipped off, sometimes in indentured servitude, often as prisoners if they resisted. They faced decades of struggle to rebuild their lives.

Those events, which happened long ago, are known as the Highland Clearances. The King of England colluded with Scottish clan chiefs to take farm land from clansmen, in order to raise sheep. Wool was in high demand.

In the contest for "most displaced," the Scots rank second only to the Israelites, though you don't hear much about it—outside of Highland pubs, where bitterness toward the English is never more than a couple of pints away.

I am not purely Scot, only half; but other branches of my family tree were shaken pretty well through history, too. My German antecedents were pacifists who left their warring land and settled in the Ukraine, when Russia's Catherine the Great promised that their children would never be conscripted. She died, the rules changed, and the peaceniks fled to the Dakota Territory.

The reasons why my French kin left the continent in the 1800s are obscure to me, but one must suppose they were hoping for something better. If work in a 19th-century New York garment factory seemed like an improvement, their lot in France must have been pretty bleak. I do not offer these snapshots of hard times as a lament. After all, the only hard times I have known have been of my own making (as have the good). My point is simply that the tides that carried our primogenitors were not always kind. But here we are, high and dry, and nothing we do today can change the currents of the past.

I wonder how many of us would, if we could?

For example, there's no question that slavery was a cruel and inhuman institution. But how many African-Americans would prefer not to live here? My guess is that the percentage is low, despite the fact that most would not be here if their great-grandparents hadn't arrived in chains. Call it acculturation, perhaps, but even with lingering discrimination and significant disparity in both wages and wealth, the personal prospects of the average nonwhite U.S. citizen are great, vis-a-vis anyplace else. That's why illegal border traffic tends to be incoming.

Or consider the Holocaust. Evil, of course. Utterly horrendous. But how many of the American Jews who fled here to escape Hitler—or, later, Stalin—are eager to return to Europe? The answer is that those from Western Europe who wanted to go home have done so. Eastern-bloc countries laid waste by World War II and despoiled during the Soviet years are not likely to be appealing destinations for anyone born in the U.S.A.

We are all here because of forces beyond our control: Get over it. Wailing and gnashing of teeth are OK if you enjoy them, but meanwhile, there's work to be done. All of us who are not Native have benefited tremendously from the happenstance that landed us here. And, truth be told, some of the Natives have done pretty well, too, though many are still in awkward recovery from genocide and future shock.

Modern humans are the descendants of Cro-Magnon folks who ate Neanderthals for breakfast. Our Australopithecan forebears probably ate Homo habilis for lunch. It's a done deal.

Enough with the angst, already. The culture that spawned the Clearances, slavery, the Holocaust and the decimation of Native America has, nonetheless, benefited the great majority. It has fed us, clothed us and educated us, notwithstanding the critical environmental damage inflicted in the process. But we have the wealth and the knowledge to attempt remediation.

The past cannot be changed, but the future can be molded. The great work of our era requires that we unite —across religious and racial lines—to address the enormity of our collective human impact on our planet.

It doesn't matter how you got here, there are mountains that have to be protected and rivers that must be restored. Prairie topsoil is eroding into the Mississippi, and smokestacks are belching toxic gases.

Pick up a shovel and shut up.

•••

Note for the current edition: Though, in the main, I still subscribe to the foregoing, I have become much more aware of white privilege in these past few years. While complaining still appears fruitless, there is much work to be done to level the playing field between the races in this country and the world.

The current buzz

If you are lucky enough to live where katydids sing a summer serenade, I wonder if you have taken time to listen to their plainsong. Musical magic echoes through the treetops in late summer, a song sixty feet deep and a thousand miles long. A song like a river. A song like a storm system swirling through hot August nights.

Katydids are leaf-green kin of grasshoppers and crickets, and like those less-eloquent cousins, they generate sound by rubbing their legs on their wings. But whereas grasshoppers make intermittent sounds, and crickets hiccup their way through a slow, "Dueling Banjos" sort of twitter, katydids are nothing short of symphonic.

When katydids mature in mid to late August, their moonlight sonata stretches from Georgia to New England. Most human ears don't sense much nuance in their calls, which someone a long time ago anthropomorphized into "Katy-did, Katy-did." A careful listener will hear more than that, however. The sound is a twittering buzz. It conveys the ping of a finger rippling tines on a stiff comb, the trill of fine bubbles in an aquarium, and something of the sibilant hiss emitted by snakes or pressure cookers.

If you climb to a promontory overlooking a mountain cove, you can apprehend the symphony in all its ululating grandeur. Swells of sound exactly like ocean waves roll through the forest canopy. The volume builds on a distant ridge and advances through the bowl of the valley, crashing around you and then continuing on.

Immersed in such wild harmony, I envision the waves beginning with a sort of jazz solo: One katydid, singing along like all the others, is suddenly moved to blast a few jubilant notes, and his immediate neighbors join in. The joyful crescendo is picked up by others, quickly building to the wave of sound that courses through the trees.

How far does that message travel? I guess it might resonate the length of the mountain chain, to the end of katydid-land, and then bounce like a boat wake off the lake shore. Think of it. One katydid in a dogwood in northeast Georgia playing a solo that reverberates in Lake Placid, New York. Another in a sugar maple overlooking Walden Pond beating out a rhythm that echoes all the way down to Roanoke, Blowing Rock, Cherokee and Chattanooga.

This is real World Music—and, like the human kind we hear on the radio, it reaches across political boundaries, linking lives. When an American slide guitarist collaborates with an Indian sitarist, a Celtic harpist tunes into Middle Eastern harmonies, a Frenchman with an electric violin joins West African drummers, or a Chinese cellist plays Mozart, there is a mixing of cultures, a cross-fertilization that changes the music, the musician and the listener. As recording technology spreads around the world, we are all increasingly exposed to the joyful noise of other lands.

What are we to make of it? What do katydids make of the vibrations from distant mountains that ripple through the night?

Maybe it's the simple message that we are not alone. Others share in katydidness and/or humanity.

Others share the dance of life, sing out in joy or suffer hardship, and find consolation in the blues.

When, someday, we hear and understand a coherent message from the stars, as one must suppose we eventually will, I wonder if it, too, will be music. I wonder if alien bodies boogie down in the light of distant suns, beat drums, blow horns and pour out their passions in song. I wonder if our answer will be a tedious political speech—or a global burst of drumming. I wonder if aliens fifty light years distant are already tuned in to Glenn Miller and Benny Goodman, while others, nearer in time and space, pick up on MTV.

I look at a katydid, its big-eyed green face as weirdly different from my own as any flying-saucer pilot's could ever be; its six legs and wings, wiggly abdomen and curved antennae unlike my own body in almost every detail. And yet I hear their music, and I get it. The world is vibrantly alive. We and they are in good company. We and they share this with the angels.

Costing cookies

Yesterday—in between pouring coffee down my gullet (to rally sleepy neurons) and corroborating the intersection of buttons and holes in my shirt (before racing out the door to follow my dashboard to town)—I heard a noise. A tiny clatter.

In the pantry.

Hmmm.

I grumbled and opened the closet door. Silence.

Appointment. Had to run. When I arrived home in the late afternoon, Susan said, "There's something in the pantry."

"I know."

"When I go in there the noise stops."

"I know."

Book in hand, I staged a stakeout, reading while I waited. At last, a tiny clatter. Aha! The cookie tin.

The lid was ajar (my doing, no doubt). When I raised the cover, I was greeted by two seed-beady and indubitably panicked eyes.

I carried the container outside and placed it on the ground, unlidded to facilitate escape. No use getting worked up about a mouse when one lives in the woods—they were here first, and they will be here long after we discorporate. The best plan is keep a lid on the cookies and other treats, and be tolerant. (The cats generally keep rodents out from underfoot, but only the black rat snakes have any effect inside the walls. The snakes, alas, are off duty in the winter.)

Others resort to poison. But, even if I were willing to visit painful death on the innocent, that plan seems shortsighted. The victims sometimes die in cavities and crevices, whence an awful stench emanates for weeks. (I've helped neighbors search.) And there is no dearth of replacements, hereabouts.

At times, we have used live traps—boxes with one-way doors, baited with peanut butter—but it's hard to feel overjoyed for the trapees. After several hours in gaol, a mouse is bathed in sweat and gasping for breath. Do our released prisoners survive after being turned out?

This morning, I went out to retrieve the cookie tin. Uh-oh. Babies. Amid the cookies and crumbs wiggled four tiny mouse pups, eyes still closed, squeaking in distress.

There is something about a large-headed, pink, wiggly, helpless little mammal that plucks at our heartstrings. This is doubtless a genetic predisposition—which curbs infanticide when human tykes are squalling, tantrumming or begging for the car keys around prom time—and genetic predispositions run very deep.

Poor things: Their situation is hopeless. Because there's no question that, by this time, Mom is off somewhere battling for her own survival, exiled from den and larder. For any species, a healthy breeding adult is more valuable, in the long run, than a baby that may never reach maturity. Those animals that produce frequent litters, like mice, place the value of individual offspring even lower. She won't be back. The kids will die.

I hasten to point out that, despite such twinges of sympathy, I would not prefer the alternative. Tolerant, yes. But five fewer mice in the house is a desirable result, even if reinforcements will arrive in due course, even if there are other litters nursing in the eaves or the cellar or behind the pantry wall at this moment. I do want to keep it down to a dull roar.

But doesn't this episode neatly illustrate the conservationist dilemma? Here is the world in a cookie tin. We need resources and space to fashion our lives and follow our dreams. We need to save the other parts as well, both for their intrinsic worth as things and beings, and for their necessary worth as part of the chain of our own survival. We need to protect our cookies. We also need to share them.

Mice are not in short supply—at least, not the white-footed, deer and harvest mice that frequent our hillside. Other creatures are. We have taken their cookies and their tins, drained their wetlands, paved their meadows, poisoned their food supplies, muddied their estuaries and chopped down their forests. Taking what we consider our fair share while our numbers swell, there is less and less to go around the table. Wolves and whales and four pink baby mice will die, to make room for my life.

How best can I, as surely I must, make room for theirs? And how high, pray tell, the price?

Exploding intentions

We live out in the sticks. Our local post office, gas station and town center are a good thirty minutes away, if one drives uncomfortably fast on curvy mountain roads. Patient drivers take forty-five.

As dedicated conservationists, we minimize our driving (and still feel guilty). Any appointment in town automatically takes in library, fuel and grocery and is apt to include the lumber yard, laundromat, auto- or tractor-parts shop and recycling station. We recognize the logical inconsistency of the would-be preservationist commuting daily from wooded countryside to urban job, pumping tons of hydrocarbons from the tailpipe of a Suburban Assault Vehicle. We usually drive the four-banger toy truck, or a tiny car. If we wanted city jobs, we would live in the city.

Enter the videocassette: temptation in a box.

Our public-library system stocks a modest collection of videos available on a two-day checkout cycle (no renewals, high fines)—three days, if you drop them into the bin before opening time, when the librarian tabulates returns. If another town trip is due in three days, it seems entirely conscionable to check out videos.

We would never drive all the way to town simply to return a movie, would we?

But there lurks a strong temptation to assume that another town trip will be warranted three days hence. Though we work at home, we are not independent homesteaders—errands happen. It's obvious that library videos could readily begin to warp our schedule into a three-day cycle. Other things that will eventually need doing can be trimmed to fit, and we could easily fool ourselves into thinking that it isn't just the videos.

Feedback is subtle. It can quietly transform attractive ideas into assumptions that guide our lives.

Take two-income households as a broader example. In mid-century America, the Norman Rockwell family included a working Dad, a full-time Mom, and their children. Mom's work was a vital part of the home economy. In addition to cooking and child-rearing chores, her gardening and canning filled the cupboards; her sewing and mending clothed the clan; and her cleaning and home maintenance were part of the job—with elder care and volunteerism, to boot.

Mobility, the sexual revolution, education, a rethinking of equality and democracy, easy divorce and other new threads appeared in our social fabric. "Woman's work" was undervalued, making the pay scale and stature of "real" jobs appealing. Expectations shifted.

What about those expectations? Though highway-linked suburbia had already suggested a second auto, the two-commuter household demanded it. Even entry-level work imposes wardrobe demands—more so for women, in a culture that rewards attractiveness. The home economy of food production and storage gave way to fast food and supermarkets.

(Not surprisingly, as the supply of workers swelled, real wages fell, though the two together were still higher than the average one had been before.)

Gradually, two wage earners became *necessary* to support new consumption patterns. Two dependable incomes led to a larger house with the second TV, the

VCR and video rentals, the computer (and the next), the new furniture, the riding (!) mower ... vacations, remodeling, golf clubs and aerobics classes ...

The day care.

Oops. One professional caregiver, however talented, cannot possibly give a half dozen or more kids (who come and go over months and years) the same focus, depth, consistency and security that a father or mother can deliver, one-on-one. The inescapable subtext for the child is that her parents have something better to do with their time. People who have something better to do with their time have no business making babies. At a minimum, a decision to parent demands an explicit agreement that at least one partner will be present and accountable during off-school hours, for the next sixteen to eighteen years.

"Affordable" day care is oxymoronic, unless a child's value is measured in dollars. Parenting is a hands-on job, and an attentive Mom or Dad inevitably tempers the creation of devalued, disaffected offspring.

To say nothing of bombs in the garage.

It's easy to pretend that we can do it all, but we can't. Something as simple as a library video schedule can undermine our best intentions. Something as complicated as a two-career household changes everything.

Working mischief, working wonders

We are wanderers, you and I, on a too-short sojourn from wasn't to isn't, on a trajectory we were thrown into, on a pathway we invent. Our footsteps are tiny, and even the most dedicated walkers among us do not travel far between birth and death. We tend to focus on the local landscape, on the immediate event, and the extent to which we see beyond depends, in large part, on the stories of others. A few have ventured up the mountain, to peer into the next valley; a few have crossed the ocean and returned; and now, a very few have looked back from space.

The world seems vast to a walker with a two-foot, two-footed stride. The sky seems high, and the oceans deep, to a two-meter being looking upward and down. Only the insight of ten thousand generations' tales can begin to instruct us in the truth of it all.

Our biosphere is a thin skin on a wee world, near a middling star in an average galaxy in a normal cluster—one among billions. It is only by the greatest good fortune that we have come to be. It is only in this one known place in the cosmos, in this one brief interval in the lengthy stretch of time, that stellar radiation and chemical recombination have erupted into life. It is only in this thin skin of air and water—no thicker than the varnish on a classroom globe—that life has emerged, photosynthesized, eaten, mated, dreamed and spoken. "We are wanderers, you and I ..."

It is only in this last, flickering moment that we wanderers have set ourselves to meddling with the biology and chemistry and nuclear forces that have balanced their own books to create our living planet. It is only in the last quarter of a moment that there have been enough of us for our meddling to have much effect. And it is only in the last blink of our eye that we have begun to understand that our numbers and our meddling can effect systemic change in the fragile bubble of life that comprises our world.

We have built our empires on petroleum—the stored energy of one hundred billion sunrises—and we're using up that energy in less than one hundred thousand days. We have permutated organic chemicals to do our bidding as pesticides, solvents and fuels, and have introduced those twisted mutagens into every living cell on earth. We have punched holes in the sky and fermented dead zones in the oceans. We have soured the rain and ripped away the topsoil where the magic of life must set root.

Perhaps we see more clearly now—and perhaps there is time for us to change. Not every kid with a chemistry set blows up the basement, after all. But the changes must be rapid—and widespread—if we are to undo our deviltry before it undoes us. The infusion of endocrine-disrupter and hormone-mimetic chemicals, which first came to broad awareness in the past decade, is endemic—and getting worse. New studies reveal a frightening correlation between pre-natal exposure and low intelligence, reduced attention span, aggression and reproductive dysfunction. To the reports of mutant frogs, homosexual seabirds, immune-deficient cetaceans, and sterile alligators we now add declining sperm count and increased testicular cancer in humans. Our chemical assault is undoing us. Basement bombs are small potatoes compared to the decoupling of our genetic freight train. There exists the possibility that the human genome project now nearing completion will finish building its Secret Decoder Ring just in time to discover that we have already monkey-wrenched the works.

Perhaps there is time for change. Indeed, we are already changing. The urge for organic food reflects a populist hunger for a step back from the brink—but the surge in SUV sales answers with a lemming-lunge for the cliff. Developing nations at long last embrace population reduction—but the U.S. government funds the development of plants that don't produce viable seeds. One step forward; two steps back.

Still wandering we are, and unsure of our goal. Once we weren't, and soon we won't be. Here in the middle, we tread our narrow path, working mischief—and working wonders.

Woo-woo versus the bunny hug

In our household, we refer to the disciplines amorphously embraced by the label "New Age" as "woo-woo." In conversation, this emerges as "She's into that woo-woo stuff," or, "Sounds pretty woo-woo to me!" This isn't meant unkindly. It is more in the way of gently humorous skepticism.

Our jocularity isn't triggered so much by the beliefs espoused as by the mercenary slant of many of the movement's practitioners. Sometimes, New Age cosmology seems like the first fundamentally mail-order religion. Madison Avenue appears to be its mecca. (Visit our Web site!)

The skepticism, however, seems more consequential.

The nontraditional folks of my acquaintance have split into two camps. On one side of the river, we see the woo-woos. Over here on my side, we practice the bunny hug.

Bunny (or tree-) hugging is the manifestation of a core belief entirely opposite that embraced by the woos. And however many attempts are made to bridge the divide, peaceful coexistence entails a large measure of good-natured tolerance.

I am no religious scholar, but I'm pretty sure this schism involves precisely the same issues that spurred

Martin Luther to nail his Ninety-Five Theses to the door of the church: Are we saved by our faith, or by our works?

In the mode du jour, I'll label the following disquisition Theses 98.

Woos clearly come down on the side of faith. I know generalizations ignore subtle wrinkles, but the bedrock remains: Woos place the inner world first and believe that changing the self will automatically change the rest.

Huggers believe in salvation through work. For us, changing the world is physical and political, and the changes in self necessary to achieve that work are also physical and political. Sacralizing work may be useful as a motive force, but in any case, the outer work must be done.

This is not to disparage the many woos who are vegetarian bicycling recyclers, nor is it to ignore the huggers who entertain deep spiritual beliefs—but the divide is as real and as deep as a river.

This difference emerged in a recent conversation with a woo of my acquaintance. We were discussing the concept of embracing abundance—the belief that the universe will provide for all of our needs if we simply open ourselves to that truth. A simple example of this would be the use of visualization to manifest a loaf of bread.

Then my friend suggested, "Existence is not a zero-sum game."

The idea here is that everyone can enjoy abundance without anyone else giving up anything. Reality is a bottomless cornucopia. We'll make more! I skidded to a halt.

"Wrong," I thought. "It is."

Here is the hurdle: If the world is not a zero-sum game, then faith alone might set us free. If it is, faith will not suffice. In a physically limited system, we need to curb our appetites and impose pollution controls.

Protecting whole watersheds and building bicycles instead of cars becomes imperative. In short, we need to work, not meditate, if reality is circular—that is, if the loops of hydrology, nutrients and energy are closed.

To the hugger, the woo embraces pretty illusions that might bring personal joy, but permit the world to die. To the woo, the hugger focuses on negative images that block personal joy—and, thus, prevent a perfect world from manifesting.

In everyday life, huggers and woos can get along, and do. Both might equally appreciate a sunny fall day, the last flowers blazing in October light, a fresh breeze off the ocean, and the spark in loving eyes. They may well agree with Alice that, at the end of the game, we can all be Kings and Queens together. But still, the divide remains. Work or faith?

Environmentalism is the philosophic stance taken by those who believe that we are doomed but might be saved by our work; therefore, the work must be done. We have no choice.

There is, of course, every possibility that we are wrong.

Pray without ceasing.

(And whistle while you work.)

II: It's breakin' my heart in two

I came here to study hard things—rock mountain and salt sea—and to temper my spirit on their edges. 'Teach me thy ways, O Lord' is, like all prayers, a rash one, and one I cannot but recommend.
-Annie Dillard
Holy the Firm

We have managed to learn some important things about the function of both the universe and ourselves.
In the universe, everything always moves ....
The planet on which we dwell continuously rotates and revolves, and the star system to which it belongs rushes through space at an unimaginably high speed....
It should be dizzying and yet we are unaware of the motion. So a second thing we have learned is that we are incapable of perceiving accurately what is happening around us. Our senses deceive us.
They bombard us with false reports....
Life is a story that each of us tells to his or herself; and it therefore is a tale told by an unreliable narrator.
-David Fromkin
The Way of the World

Look both ways

I have previously confessed that I brake for turtles. When I see one crossing the road, I stop and help it on its way.

Last summer, I pulled over and stepped out of my truck, intent on rescuing a handsome, yellow-and-black box turtle. Instead I watched, helpless, as another truck sped by and smashed it into the pavement. Blood and organs were splattered amid a pile of crushed shell. I felt nauseated, riven by a fundamental sense of injustice at the death of a stalwart creature who had crawled through fifty years of summer heat and winter hibernation to end up in the wrong place at the wrong time. I seethed with anger at the driver who hadn't even tried to miss the plodding reptile. Once again—and intensely—I connected with the sense of loss that's always sitting on my shoulder, ever ready to whisper Dante's lament, "Abandon hope."

The things I love are dying.

I don't suppose that desolate feeling will go away. In fact, the next thirty years of my life will probably make the last thirty seem like a party, as our planet is crushed beneath wildly proliferating human numbers.

Once, I gazed out from my house at nighttime darkness; now, more than a dozen porch lamps and security lights have crept up the valley. Not long ago, I awoke to morning bird calls in the quiet breeze; now, barking dogs and machine sounds filter even into dawn. The farm at the foot of my hill has been subdivided and subdivided again. Roads have been widened, woods have been cut, traffic has increased. Litter, smoke, horns, sirens, jets and helicopters and friendly realtors bearing beckoning signs sidle ever closer.

They tell me that my home gains in value when more houses spring up nearby. They don't remotely comprehend that the only value that makes any sense to me is being destroyed forever.

The same week I saw the turtle killed, I received a phone call from a person upset about bears. It seems that a mother and three cubs had been getting into her garbage, and she wanted someone to remove the offending beasts. My best suggestion was to build a sturdier garbage enclosure or haul it away more frequently. Both ideas were rejected. The family doesn't have time. They can't afford it.

Since meat scraps are the strongest garbage lure for bears, the simplest solution would be to stop eating dead animals. But having offered that idea to folks in the past, I know it is a non-starter.

The problem is not bears—it is people moving into bear territory. This person's land backs up to national-forest land. Where else could you possibly take bears to give them a chance to survive? Why move to the edge of wild land and then complain about the wild?

Polls suggest that most folks want to protect the environment. Do they imagine we can save the whole without saving all of the pieces?

A constant sense of loss. Reintroduced wolves are shot. Japan resumes whaling. The governor wants more highways. Hog farms poison rivers. Another oil spill. Another baby every other second. Dogwoods, spruce, hemlocks and beeches are dying. Detroit makes bigger cars that use more fuel because an "environmentalist" nation demands sport-utility vehicles—to drive more miles into more wild places, to plant more lawns to spray with more diazinon. Put the bears in a zoo: bottled wildlife watching people drinking bottled water. Let them eat cake.

I saw a green snake this summer—a first for me in the Carolinas—about sixty seconds after it was disemboweled by a car tire. Sic transit.

I try to harden my shell and get beyond the pavement that surrounds. I try to nurture hope. "See this! There is beauty here! There is life!" But the rampant machine looms large and fast, fueled by ideas and purposes that don't include me. My very hope seems puny and slow, feeble dreams of a 46-year-old, bony bubble stranded on life's highway—unsure whether to tuck or run.

Three days later, I saw that turtle again—just a stain on the pavement, and a few bits of shell. No one coming after will even recognize that tiny tragedy.

No one coming after will know.

Dark enough to see

The stars are brighter in wild places. Perhaps thoughts are clearer, as well, though that is a personal bias and not the sort of phenomenon that lends itself to scientific inquiry. Still, far from glaring electric signs, street lights, billboards, beacons and headlights, the night is different. The Milky Way washes the sky, and a thousand diamond flares become a million.

I live on a rural ridge. Visitors from the city are often amazed when they step out on my deck after dark. With only a dozen or so porch lamps and security lights visible in the valley below, the closest at least a mile distant, the stars seem clear and the sky black. It's easy for me to forget how much my view has been clouded by the electric fog all around. Easy, that is, until I go someplace deeper and richer and farther from civilization's visual noise.

Not long ago, night found me in the relative seclusion of a quiet beach on a sleepy bay. I looked up to see the firmament I remember from my childhood—and wanted to weep for all that has been lost. The constellations are still there, the figures of Greek or Native American myth. It is our vision that has dimmed. There are stars between the stars I see at home, and stars between those, as well. I was filled again with wonder at the infinite splendor that surrounds us—and devastated by our rush to replace the blackness with shades of grey.

Security lights.

Ha. As if light provided any security at all. Put a garish, orangey-pink fire on a totem pole in your driveway, and you will be safe! The boogeyman won't get you! More news at eleven. Tales of murder and mayhem, and the vain hope that it will all go away if we only get rid of the darkness. A billion watts later, do you feel more secure?

Street lights and more street lights, to make the streets safe. Stand a pole up every mile, every half mile, every quarter, every corner, everywhere. Light makes everyone sane and sober. Maniacs are creatures of shadow. You will make it home in one piece, because the lights are on.

Count the billboards illuminated by carbon-arc beacons, one after another along the highway berm. Bright and bright and brighter. Buy me. Stop here. Eat this. Consume and consume as we consume the sky. Forget your sense of wonder at the marvel of the universe —the real stars are on TV. Laugh and laugh and forget the fear. More news at eleven. Tales of murder and mayhem, and the vain hope that it will all go away if we only get rid of the darkness.

No wonder the gods feel forgotten in the brightness that surrounds us. Our smallness is forgotten, too. We are big and bright, and we can make even the stars disappear. Everything that matters is here and now and on the screen. The bright screen, with bright smiles and problems that all resolve in a half hour (or ninety minutes, for serious drama).

Yes, it is an electric age. The lights reflect on clouds of soot from generator stacks. Rivers are stopped and turbined, their juice diverted to electrify the streets. Nuclear stations pump it up, pump it up, and keep piling on the radioactive waste, with still no solution in sight.

Forget about the waste-disposal problem—it will be solved, because we are powerful. Powerful enough to take away the darkness, to hide the stars, to hide the fear, to hide from God.

But the problems that can't be solved between ads and canned laughter on a sitcom stage are still there, in the dusk. The atmosphere is changing, as are the oceans and rivers and deserts. Spent nuclear fuel lurks in temporary facilities, awaiting a disposal fix that may never come. And who we are, where we are from, and where we are bound—the riddles of the ages—are still adrift in the murky sea of the unconscious. Turn on every light in the world, hide the stars, hide the night—but the big ones are still waiting.

On that quiet beach—far from the city, and far from my home—I heard the stars sing. We cannot change the universe; the universe changes us. The light of a million-billion watts still pales before the light of a trillion suns.

Whirl away

I am not a real birder. No "life list" of myriad species observed. No journeys around the world to spy endangered rarities. And I am terrible at remembering calls—barring a few blatantly distinctive exceptions, most of the twitters, whistles and clicks that birds utter leave me clueless.

But I love to watch, floating downriver in a canoe—beer in one hand, binoculars in the other, steering-paddle tucked under my arm—keenly alert to the wild things all about.

There's a red-shouldered hawk perched atop a dead palm trunk, tearing at the unseen prey pinned in its claws. Chunks of wet, red something, ripped and swallowed. A white-spotted brown limpkin wails like a banshee, then resumes poking its long, downturned beak between weeds, in search of apple snails. Now a dull grey eastern phoebe zooms overhead, stalls for two beats and veers to a nearby branch, its twitching breakfast bug briefly visible. And gone.

Unless you spot birds engaged in courtship or building nests, their primary interesting activity is eating. Birdseed is big business, no? Not so different from us, really: We woo. We find housing. We eat. And, having those three squares passably covered for the moment, Susan and I are back in the canoe again, watching.

The present journey has been more than usually colored by death—always there, to be sure, but this time not easily ignored. An American alligator floating upside down in the weeds, and a river otter similarly positioned against a drifting log, attest to someone's able, if misguided, marksmanship. A young grey fox showing no apparent fatal wound lies stiff amid pine needles, which still bear the imprint of its final contortions. And, strangest of all, beneath four feet of clear, flowing water, a white-tailed doe.

We paddle back over her, wait for ripples to flatten, and look again. Completely intact: Two forelegs hooked around a submerged branch kick languidly in the current. Her head is thrown back, and she lies belly up, little teats attesting to her gender. We guess she has not been dead long, else the gators and turtles would have parted her out.

But there are other shadows, too: Each of us has a mother's sister enduring untender cancer therapy. We are all terminal. Some of us are led to believe that we've been more specifically informed, but no matter. We each owe the earth one body—our tuppence for the piper who has favored us with this lovely tune, this wondrous dance.

Dust to dust. Geologist Vladimir Ivanovitch Vernadsky referred to life as a "disperse of rock." We are not separate from the earth's crust, Vernadsky observed, we are just the parts that visibly wiggle. Agitated molecules whirling into dervishes, CEOs, peasant farmers and canoe paddlers. Moving, always moving...

And what motion! Vultures, both black and turkey, soar together overhead. Up and up into the yonder, till binoculars are insufficient to follow their flight. Searching for leftovers and riding the wind. Nice work if you can get it—perfect players in the recycling loop, probate jurists in this mineral disperse.

Apart from the buzzards (and headed higher), an adult bald eagle, wings stiff as twin ironing boards, circles above a juvenile baldy practicing her moves. I once met a woman who hang-glides for sport; she recalled rising impossibly high on an updraft above Mount Shasta— wingtip to wingtip with our national bird. She said the eagle first seemed curious about the Dacron-fledged interloper in its airspace, but presently grew bored and moved on. Up.

I look up. There, atop a bleached pine snag, sits a vigilant osprey, black talons biting into pale wood. I aim my binoculars and am startled by the view. Above the feathered shoulder hangs the waxing, gibbous moon, a semicircular mirage set in aching blue. Wondering under my gaze, the bird's head pivots, and together, we consider the familiar lunar image.

The osprey turns back with a shrug. "Oh, that." Nothing there but dust. No water there for dancers to drink. The party never even got started.

Here on terra firma, though, the party never ends. I eat another boiled peanut, sip my beer, and watch four eastern painted sliders plop off a log. Miracle after miracle, we celebrate, we whirl.

•••

Note for the current edition: Ten years have passed since the canoe trip described above and this remains one of my favorite essays. A decade brings change, of course, and I look back from a rather different vantage point. Three years later it was Susan's turn to confront a cancer diagnosis, and in two more she succumbed. But we, the parts still wiggling, continue to celebrate and whirl.

On a wing and a prayer

Last August, we had out-of-state visitors on our ridge. They were impressed with the beauty of the Appalachian Mountains, enjoying the relative cool above three thousand feet. But their highest praise and loudest exclamations were reserved for the insects.

"So many butterflies!" they exclaimed.

Fair enough. We do enjoy a great diversity of beautiful butterflies. And, if that had been their only comment, you might think we just happen to have more members of the order Lepidoptera here than they do back in flatland. But listen to the next line:

"I haven't seen so many since I was a child!" said one. "We don't have butterflies like these anymore," lamented another.

Do you hear the drumbeat of death in those words? No? Well, you should. A slow change moves across the land, and it is, at minimum, profound and disturbing. It may be a catastrophe.

Pollinator populations are collapsing in many places around the world. The insects, birds and mammals that fertilize flowers by transferring pollen from one to the next are in sharp decline. Last year, the disappearance of honeybees in the Midwest and the Carolinas made the news, but honeybees are only the most familiar of the pollinator species.

Without pollination, we and the rest of the animals on earth would soon lose our lunches. And our breakfasts and dinners. Most flowering plants need help with fertilizing seeds, and the animal forms that have co-evolved with them do the job perfectly. There are butterflies and moths with long probosci that can reach deep into tubular flowers, and hummingbirds with a similarly extended reach. Many varieties of bats pollinate night-blooming flowers while feeding on their nectar. And thousands of species of bees—from tiny, bright-colored sweat bees to the huge, dark carpenter sort—move pollen grains from anther to stigma on weeds and trees and orchids and peas. There are beetles and ants and even mosquitos who each have an important role to play.

In many cases, flowers and the critters that fertilize them are tightly entwined, one-on-one, so that neither can survive without the other. Others may depend on just a few species of plants or animals. And, in every case, they're part of the great chain of life that created and maintains the living world we all inhabit.

But back to those butterflies: Why did my guests react so strongly? They live in Ohio, in a residential area between a city and surrounding farms. Because of pesticide sprays on lawns and fields, wild insects and flowers have disappeared. Many of the plants that sustain butterflies and moths are considered weeds and are subject to eradication programs.

On top of the chemical assault, habitats are fragmented by cleared fields and lawns that replace native vegetation with imported monocultures. If a butterfly—or a hummingbird or bat, for that matter—can't find a high enough concentration of food in an area, it will move on, or starve to death.

The problem would be merely aesthetic, if all we lost were life forms that we find beautiful and appealing. But our understanding of the web of life is still rudimentary, at best. We have only a sketchy appreciation of the intricacy of plant-and-animal interactions that maintain soil fertility, atmospheric oxygen levels, water purity and other chemical systems that are the foundation of all life. We know that humans cannot exist alone, without any other species—but we have no clue which species those essential friends might be. Pollination is the crucial juncture for all flowering plants, and the disappearance of pollinator animals will impact our lives in ways we cannot foresee. Yet we continue to abet an extinction spasm that will take hundreds or thousands of species of critters and plants out of the loop forever.

You can help. Encourage weeds and wildflowers. Let part of your lawn go wild. Learn to live with wasps and bees and beetles and ants and even mosquitos. Repel insects with screens, long sleeves or incense, instead of killing them. If you garden, choose organic controls. In silviculture, avoid herbicides, and allow space for mixed stands. Oppose clearcuts. Remind others of the vital services living systems provide us, and the urgent need to protect whole, natural communities. Learn more by contacting the Migratory Pollinators Program, <http://www.desertmuseum.org/pollination/> or the North American Pollinator Protection Campaign, <http://www.nappc.org/>.

If you marvel that a fragile monarch butterfly can migrate thousands of miles, or that a delicate swallowtail can survive a tornado, remember this: Those tissue-paper wings very likely carry our own future, too.

•••

Note for the current edition: This was written almost a decade before the current honeybee problem emerged. Colony Collapse Disorder has raised the stakes for pollinators and animals that enjoy regular meals.

Trapped

Ten years ago, in *The End of Nature* (Random House, 1989), author Bill McKibben pointed out that there is no longer a wild world unaffected by human decisions. The remaining bits and pieces that are more or less wild exist only where we let them, and most of the habitable acreage on the planet is managed for our economic benefit. The upshot of this is that we confront constant management decisions.

Viewed at the most local level, such supervision involves what we eat, what chemicals we use or eschew in our homes and gardens, and what flora and fauna we permit or encourage. Do you value spiders for insect-control, and snakes because they eat rodents, or do you destroy them because of a subliminal, neurotic fear? Are caterpillar-consuming wasps a garden ally or a threat? Do you consider dandelions to be wildflowers or weeds?

As a society, we embrace the idea of preserving parts of the natural world in parks and reserves, but the question of what deserves protection, and how best to achieve that end, is an ethical and political minefield. Presently, the management of two related species neatly illustrates the prickliness of this dilemma.

If you take pleasure in the natural world as image or idea, you probably find wolves and foxes appealing. These beautiful creatures fill important eco-niches and resonate in fables and literature. The quick brown fox lives on in most typists' first sentences. *Little Red Riding Hood* and *The Call of the Wild* resonate in our dreams. Statistically, the chances are good that you oppose trapping these animals for their fur. But what about trapping, per se?

Wolves have been reintroduced into Yellowstone and Great Smoky Mountains national parks, parts of Idaho, Arizona and New Mexico. The results have ranged from great success in Yellowstone to failure in the Smokies. Where this effort is working, it has helped restore a natural balance destroyed by human extermination efforts over the last two centuries. Ungulate populations have been reduced so that more tree seedlings survive, coyotes have been knocked from the top eco-slot they assume in the wolf's absence, and the whole food chain, from insects to grizzlies, is re-balancing at a more "natural" level. But the wolves obtained for these projects were trapped for relocation, and are regularly recaptured for veterinary evaluation, using a gentler variant of the infamous leg-hold trap.

The situation is reversed in California, where foxes were introduced by humans in the late 1800s. The foxes have prospered and are now considered the primary threat to numerous ground-nesting birds that face extinction. The only way to save the endangered birds is to eliminate the foxes. But, according to wildlife experts, the only practical way to eliminate the foxes is to trap them, and there is no fox-free habitat available for re-location.

Tough call. Wildflower or weed? What is natural? Do we manage the wild world to re-create the status quo in 1990, or 1890, or 9090 B.C.E.? Is the right model for North America the pre-Columbian or the pre-Native? Mongolian invaders wiped out the woolly mammoth and the giant sloth; European interlopers wiped out the woodland buffalo and the passenger pigeon. If we attempt to stop the clock today, by simply "letting nature take its course" without intentional human management, the evidence is that we are headed for Weed World. Urban-adaptive animals like coyotes, foxes, starlings, pigeons, rabbits and cockroaches will prosper. Purple loosestrife will conquer our wetlands. Lampreys and zebra mussels will rule the Great Lakes, and red tide and pfisteria will sour the sea. The total number of species, already extincting at a record pace, will collapse ever faster.

The meta-trap in which we are caught is of our own devising. In just half a century, our numbers have exploded (and may double again, before we get a grip). The only large vertebrate or tree species that survive our onslaught will be the ones we choose to protect, or fail to control. Like it or not, we are Caesar, and the world is our Coliseum. Thumbs up? Thumbs down? The combatants' lives depend utterly upon our resolve.

Seeing trees in the forest

Forest ecosystems are collapsing. There is probably no more important news you will hear in your lifetime—but, chances are, you haven't heard much about it. In the United States, the story has been buried, along with information about global warming, by coal and oil companies and their allies. They attempt to muddle the facts and block even modest attempts to fix our serious environmental problems.

Before you write me off as a nut case prone to hollering "wolf," I suggest you take a walk in the woods. Find out for yourself what is happening to the plants you depend on for every breath you take.

If you start your walk on top of North Carolina's Mount Mitchell, there aren't any woods to walk in, anymore. Acid precipitation wiped out the spruce forest a decade ago. Perhaps you could try Mount Rogers, in western Virginia, where the northern hardwoods are going fast. Then drive along the Blue Ridge Parkway and notice the dying tops of maples and beeches all along your route. Lower still, look at the wrinkled bark of dead dogwoods and the lesions and shelf fungi on locust trees. Even if you have never considered tree health before in your life, you can't miss the symptoms.

Count the trees on an acre, and note how many are standing, but dead. Normal mortality in a maple forest, for example, should be about one percent per year, with about seven percent standing dead. This makes sense, if you consider that maples may live for one hundred or more years. Most of the trees should exhibit vigorous health. Most of the trees do not.

A forester I spoke with in Vermont told me that, in vast sections of that state, there are no healthy trees at all. We took a short walk, and on one tree after another, he pointed out the stigmata of decline. In the past decade, he observed, the failure of his woods had been gradual, but now the change is becoming exponential. He wondered aloud if his trees would last another five years.

A University of Tennessee researcher, who has studied tree decline, tells people that if they want to see the magnificent northern-hardwood forests in the Southern Appalachians, they'd better hurry.

And even if the trees were in excellent health, the planet is getting warmer fast—very fast. To survive in a warmer world, species must move north, or uphill. Trees move very slowly, since they must mature and produce a crop of seeds which then, hopefully, sprout in a more favorable location. Each degree of warming means plants must move forty miles north, or sixty feet up slope. But parts of northern Ontario have already warmed by three degrees within the last decade, and acid precipitation is most serious at high elevations. The situation is extremely bleak.

What can be done? Powerful, monied interests recommend that we simply keep studying the situation. The oil and coal companies treat us to a repetitive litany from a handful of well-paid professional doubters. If we follow their lead, we will literally study the question to death.

Meanwhile, Republicans in Congress say, "Yes, let's study it more," and then cancel funding for the research they claim we need.

We don't have to relinquish the future; there is work to be done. We can become a renewable, solar economy instead of a fossil-fuel and nuclear dead end—a true service economy, instead of a society of mindless consumers. Insulate, insulate, insulate—and then, heat with wood, instead of oil or coal. This recycles currently free carbon, whereas fossil fuels release carbon that's been chemically locked out of the atmosphere for thousands of years. Natural gas is the cleanest choice, if you can't burn wood. Drive fewer, slower miles. Ride your bike. Use less electricity. Buy local farm products. Tell your family. Tell your neighbor. Tell elected officials.

Remember that the money the oil companies use to buy political and media influence comes from you. The only power they have derives from our wallets, and our wallets are still in our hands.

It's entirely possible that a worldwide populist movement toward sustainability can succeed. There is no better place to start than here. There is no better time than now.

Let us begin.

•••

Note for the current edition: Perhaps there is room for hope now that the Bush administration is careening toward an end. The rest of the world seems to be holding its breath, waiting for us to depose the blindered prince. At the national policy level, the years since I wrote this essay have been all but wasted.

Scaling hope

Seen at full scale, the global situation seems hopelessly bleak. Count it among our blessings that the world is round—the near horizon moderates our view of the catastrophic.

Then, too, our minds are more comfortable with the immediate and tiny than with distant hugeness. We easily consider glasses half-drained, but experience some trouble when it comes to aquifers and fisheries. Such mental delimitation may result from evolution on this horizon-bound world. And, in any case, the mastodon about to plant a tusk in one's belly has always been a more effective attention-getter than the enumeration of fish in the seven seas, or of ice crystals in Antarctica.

But I've been dwelling on bigger pictures lately, feeling a little boggled and a little blue.

Ten years ago, Valdez became a household word when that tanker ruptured and disgorged its viscous cargo in Prince William Sound. Dead animals, idle fishing boats, briefed lawyers, de-briefed sailors, disquieting headlines, accusations and counter-accusations followed. A royal mess.

I once discovered a beached seal, suffocated in oil on the Olympic coast. Its eyes, nose, mouth, fur, fins and tail were coated with a thick, black sludge. One dead animal is a grasp-able concept that I might extrapolate to thousands, while viewing pictures of the Alaska debacle—though, even so, the numbers quickly blur. In the same way, over in the other Washington, I see the face of that boy in my high-school class when I gaze down the length of a black-marble wall, the particular Vietnam casualty set against the incomprehensible mass horror. I know but I don't know. Perhaps I simply can't.

Try this: The length of coastline inundated in Prince William Sound is roughly the length of the Atlantic coast, from Miami to New York. "Oh," you may say.

If the latter seems more tangible, it's partly familiarity, and partly our maps. (The generic Mercator projection shrinks polar regions and expands the middle lattitudes—useful for captains more likely to ply temperate waters than Alaskan seas.)

Now try this: The Valdez spill is only the 53rd largest we have seen.

So far.

Now this: A single Chinese seafood market sells five thousand turtles per day—more than one-and-a-half million per year. There are many markets. The Chinese believe that consumption of turtles promotes longevity. In the past decade, Asia's turtle population has collapsed underneath this superstition-driven onslaught. Suppliers have fanned out to mine the world's supply. In a past column, I lamented the crushing of one box turtle beneath an unswerving truck tire—a laughable microcosm. Because turtles, writ large, are being crushed by a very real Yellow Peril, and extinction of most species looms. The appetite, it seems, is unswerving.

But why fasten on such paltry cravings? Terrapin-extincting gastronomy is but a teardrop in the ocean, compared to humanity's hunger for wood and water, grain and fiber.

One-quarter of the world's forests have disappeared since I was born, in 1950. Logging is on the rise. Humans use or divert more than half the liquid fresh water on earth—and, in consequence, one-third to three-quarters of the freshwater fish species on each continent are threatened or endangered. We produce and consume about 1.7 billion tons of grain annually, though per-capita production is about what it was in 1966 (and falling). Grain stocks are at an all-time low. (Try to imagine ten tons of wheat in a large dump truck; now, visualize 170 million of them driving by, while 6 million humans starve to death—each year.) Those of us who can afford luxury array ourselves in cotton (doused annually with 250 million pounds of pesticides, in this country alone); others make do with polyester—and it seems that we're right back to the tankers again.

The very-rich wrap their infants in disposable diapers, woven from the pulped trunks of eight-hundred-year-old hemlocks—trees sprouted back in the Dark Ages, not to be seen by we enlightened ones again.

Meanwhile, in the time it takes you to read this sentence, the world's human population will increase by twenty-four. In the time it took me to write this essay, another species has gone extinct. Considered too deeply, this is the stuff of lemminghood, so we do what we can to salvage sundry pieces. But our response has been/is/will be insufficient.

Hope seems irrational, but then, rationality has never been our strong suit.

Hope.

•••

Note for the current edition: It's now nearing two decades since the Valdez disaster. Exxon continues to stonewall on its financial obligation while it continues to garner obscene profits. When I interviewed environmental educator David Orr in the fall of 2007, I found he had reached much the same conclusion. "Optimism is irrational," he told me. "Pessimism is unproductive. Humans can be heroic , all we can do is hope for heroism."

III. Until you use me up

It is important to conserve biodiversity not because it may be useful or profitable (though in some cases it will be), but because in the act of conserving we will begin to save ourselves from what has become an all-engulfing planetary nihilism, one that ultimately threatens humankind itself. Conservation is not just about conserving different species, or conserving different human cultures, but about making possible different futures and different worlds. It is a foundational act of freedom—
.   *for ourselves and other beings.*
.   **-Bruce Rich**
Mortgaging the Earth

To fly to the sun without burning a wing,
to lie in the meadow and hear the grass sing,
To have all these things in our memory store,
and to use them,
to help us ...
-Graeme Edge
Departure

Stone tablets and all that

We've all heard lots of environmental advice, from "Fifty things you can do to save the planet" to "Think globally, act locally." All of it is useful, and to varying degrees, it has helped begin to steer us toward sustainability.

Lately, however, John Huie—director of the Environmental Leadership Center of Warren Wilson College—challenged me to take a fresh look at how we can work for change, and then distill the answer into a few basic maxims.

I think his idea was that fifty rules are a lot to remember, and thinking globally may seem somewhat amorphous. At the end of a difficult work day—when you're facing a dozen dreary errands before speeding home to throw together supper for the family, and you discover that the car battery's dead—how many of us calmly assume a big-picture perspective?

Herewith, then, are my Three Commandments for Treading Lightly on the Earth: 1. Make fewer feet. 2. Downsize your footprint. 3. Upgrade your path.

"Make fewer feet," means "avoid procreation." Population growth is the bottom line on environmental impact. It is impossible to stop the destruction of the natural world that supports us if we don't reign in our numbers. This is more urgent in industrialized nations than in developing ones, because of our enormous resource use.

We must advocate childlessness and laws that encourage tiny families: Tax deductions for children should end at two, and women who remain childless past menopause—or any adult who chooses voluntary sterilization—should get a double deduction.

If you feel uncontrollably compelled to parent, delay your atavistic urges as long as biologically possible. Note that children of older parents tend to be better adjusted psychologically and brighter students than those born to youngsters.

Next, "Downsize your footprint." This rule covers a lot of the usual ground. Reduce, re-use, recycle. Eat lower on the food chain. Vegetarianism cuts air and water pollution and saves trees, fossil fuels, electricity—and your health. A meat-based diet requires twenty times as much farm land as a vegan one.

Be frugal. First, reduce daily fuel and material use; then, delay replacing durable goods. Put off buying a new car or appliance as long as possible. Adopt the zen of timely maintenance.

Finally, I suggest, "Upgrade your path." I think I'm on new ground with this one. Sometimes, all the talk about a Spartan future begins to sound pretty bleak. This rule should make saving the Earth seem a little less depressing. It is meant to remind you that a wine connoisseur doesn't drink more than a wino—more likely, the opposite is true—but the connoisseur drinks better wine.

Buy fewer but higher-quality goods. The resources used to make a crummy screwdriver are about the same as for a high-quality tool, but the good one will create enormous savings over its longer life. The same is true of clothing, cars and kitchenware. Don't use disposables. Drinking from a styrofoam cup is not even in same league with stoneware mugs or crystal stemware. In the one lifetime you are inarguably guaranteed, why waste the chance for elegance? Ritzy restaurants don't use paper napkins—why do it at home?

You can upgrade your path to be a philosopher instead of a consumer. That is, you can collect ideas instead of objects, you can create beauty instead of garbage.

Let's apply that to our hypothetical problem. Rule one means you'd have fewer child-oriented errands and meals, and more free time after work. Rules one and two mean your overall budget is lower, so you could restructure your life around a shorter work week. And, thanks to rule three, you bought a five-year battery instead of a 24-month one, so your car starts right up. Less shopping and fewer work days mean fewer miles on your car, which will last well into the next century, when you finally recycle it and get a solar-powered sports car— or a mountain bike.

So, that's it. Make fewer feet. Downsize your footprint. Upgrade your path. A sustainable culture is as easy as one, two, three. We don't have to follow consumerism's cheerleaders over a cliff, like a herd of greedy little lemmings. Instead, we can build a society in which kindness and a sense of our planetary interdependence shine brighter than gold.

Dinosaur juice

Sinclair Oil adopted a cartoon brontosaurus as its mascot several decades ago, popularizing the idea that petroleum is composed of dead thunder lizards. But there's a great deal more significance in that simple notion than most folks bother to note: The implications, indeed, are profound.

Of course, oil is not simply dinosaur juice. It is equally an agglomeration of giant ferns and tree club mosses, dragonflies and cockroaches, trilobites and fish and squids, bacteria, algae and slime molds. Petroleum is a chemical cocktail of complex hydrocarbons assembled by living cells, accumulated over vast expanses of time. The decayed organic matter that is the central material resource of modern culture is the result of millions of centuries of life on Earth.

Take a moment to try to grasp that thought. Millions of centuries represents a passage that's almost impossible to comprehend. Our whole story of civilization could be replayed one hundred thousand times in that stretch. During those eons, the continents have separated and collided in their dance around the planet. Yet, in a very real sense, what we now call oil is an embodiment of that immense span, measured in accumulated photosynthesis, digestion and growth.

Now, consider that, in less than one hundred years, we have used up most of our oil. In twenty more, the supply will be sharply dwindling. In fifty or so, it will be gone as a commercially meaningful resource. By 2015, about eighty percent of the known oil reserves will be gone—and our human population will be headed toward ten billion.

But, by then, we'll discover alternatives, right? For energy, yes. Solar, wind, tidal, geothermal, natural gas, hydroelectric, coal and nuclear power have the potential to fill the electric void. The first half of that list is more benign than the latter, but they will all figure in our future power supply.

Replacing oil's other uses, however, is far more problematic. As writer Thomas Berry has noted, it is extremely difficult to visualize modern Western civilization sans petroleum. Look around you: Plastic, fabric, numerous pharmaceuticals, lubricants, fertilizer, pesticides, paint, tires and the roads they roll on are all petrochemical products. And alternatives to these other uses of oil are surprisingly scarce. Plastic from corn cobs? Fine, but what about the fertilizer for the corn?

In fact, it is fertilizer that will probably demand the most sweeping changes in our habit patterns. In the short run, natural-gas derivatives can meet part of the need for plant food, but this resource, too, is limited and will be in high demand for fuel as the oil runs out.

An obvious source of nutrient material is manure—ours. But consider the enormity of the undertaking! Modern plumbing has removed us from the natural loop of plant to animal to manure to plant. Closing that cycle on a meaningful scale will entail what may be the largest public-works project ever attempted. Inventor Gerry Hawkes has suggested that the most practicable method might involve switching to composting toilets and instituting a regular collection service. This would also avoid the difficulties today's sewer systems create by adding water and chemical pollution to these wastes. Such a change, of course, would require a massive amount of money and time, yet I am unaware of any government body which has even considered such an option. Some municipalities do compost their sewage sludge, but the industrial-toxin-laden goop is unsafe for use on food crops.

Another obvious choice involves hemp. With its lower requirements for fertilizer and pesticides than other fiber and food crops, it reduces agricultural dependence on petroleum. At the same time, hemp-seed oil can fill many of the resource niches that are now petro-based. Politically, however, hemp has been a hard sell, and even after governments eventually get with the program, a switch in crops, processing machinery and industrial methods could take decades.

The lesson that oil can teach us is simple, but non-obvious: Life comes from life. Oil is not a dead thing; it is the product of eons of organic growth, death and rebirth. Replacements for petroleum will come from living matter as well, and the pending scarcity will inestimably affect the lives of all of us.

Water fights

I have friends who live in a small, rural enclave with a community well. Originally developed twenty years ago as a second-home vacation retreat, a combination of nearby urban growth and housing shortages has helped transform the neighborhood into a primary residential community. But the influx of full-timers has suddenly altered the social consonance involved in sharing, and the eight cabin owners now confront a global problem writ small. Though the well is used and maintained in common, the property developer did not attach ownership of the water source to deeds. In other words, while all have enjoyed its use, none has a legal claim. The situation reverberates with issues we all face on a far larger scale: A commons enjoyed, shared and protected by consensus is highly subject to abuse.

When the first buyers purchased their cool summer retreats, they didn't look too hard at how well their water supply was winter-proofed. They were content to know that the plumbing worked during their two-week summer vacations or leaf-looking visits in fall. The first crisis emerged when one resident tried to keep an inadequately insulated tank and shallowly laid pipes going through the winter. Who would pay for ice-shattered pipes (which had been drained in earlier winters)? Should all of the pipe be reburied below the frost line? What about the electric bill for a heater in the pump house, where none had been needed before?

Years later, the five-hundred-gallon reservoir rusted out, and the water-system manager (a non-resident old-timer), working within a meager budget funded by voluntary dues, opted for a smaller pressure tank. Unfortunately, the lower dynamic volume provides less elasticity when demand is high.

More folks moved in, nudging the system along toward its quick-recovery limits; and, last week, a wild card turned up. An uphill cabin owner decided he needed more water pressure and turned down the valves regulating his downhill neighbors' supplies. Discovering inadequate pressure, the others soon re-opened their lines, and Guy Uphill responded in kind. In the next round, Uphill found his valve completely turned off—so he padlocked it open. The others will, presumably, have to do likewise, and it will surprise no one if the whole mess ends up in court (or in fisticuffs).

In the wider world, too, this scenario is playing out with increasing frequency, as ready sources of fresh water are tapped, diverted and even exhausted. Turkey, which controls the headwaters of the Tigris and Euphrates rivers, quietly announced plans to dam those arteries of history's Fertile Crescent. Iran and Syria loudly responded that they would consider that an act of war. U.S. engineers hatched a plan to purchase and divert Canadian rivers to feed the parched American West, bringing howls of protest from our northern neighbor. More recently, plans to haul tankers-ful of Great Lakes water to Southeast Asian markets have drawn fire on both sides of the Canadian border. Meanwhile, on the other side of Big Blue, Soviet central planners managed to destroy the Aral Sea, wiping out its fisheries and nearby agricultural areas, by shunting major tributaries into irrigation systems.

Conflicts between individual nations may be resolved by the World Court, or by laser-guided bombs, but the larger issue will remain. Ninety million new full-time residents arrive on our little globe each year, and we will have half again as many thirsty neighbors, in thirty years' time. The supply system is being pushed toward its limits, and the shrinking per-capita reservoirs are far less elastic.

As we prepare to swan-dive into the birth-boom looming on our near horizon, a wild card has turned up—the Earth is warming. How much and how fast our weather might change remains a computer-modeled guessing game, but already the oceans are rising, deserts are expanding, rain forests are drying, and precipitation is trending toward extremes of gully-washing and drought.

The bumper sticker on the car ahead reads, "We all live downstream," and that's true in the broadest sense. But some of us are more downstream than others. Prudence suggests that down-river folk could do worse than to take Guy Uphill a piece of pie now and again, and Uphill might do well to consider a padlock. The squabbling has barely begun.

The horse's mouth

Charity can be an iffy business, in the best of circumstances. It's not always easy to identify the needy as well as the need, and to sort out causes and effects. I'm reminded of a letter from a teacher in the Philippines expressing gratitude for computers provided to her school, but suggesting that sanitary toilets were a more pressing problem. And so it goes.

The Christmas shopping season offers charitable groups excellent leverage in the form of latent guilt about over-consumption. I recently learned about one such effort, which neatly frames the eleemosynary conundrum.

The Heifer Project International solicits funds to provide livestock to poor families around the globe. For a contribution of twenty to five hundred dollars, one can give a flock of chicks or ducks, a sheep or a goat, a camel, llama or cow—with the stipulation that the recipient, in turn, must give one female offspring to another needy villager. On the face of it, this appears to be an ideal gift— the sort that keeps on giving.

But look again.

A good place to start would be sub-Saharan Africa in the 1960s. In an effort to improve living conditions for farmers of arid land, World Bank planners made drilling water wells a high priority. The need for dependable water sources was self-evident, wasn't it? But the unforeseen result was a massive increase in cattle herds—which, naturally, were clustered near the wells, where they over-grazed surrounding land and contributed to subsequent famine. Oops.

In retrospect, it's easy to see that liquidity—literal, in this case—would lead to investment in stocks—live-, in this case—in a culture in which cattle are the primary form of wealth.

Agronomist Masanobu Fukuoka, author of *The One Straw Revolution* and other books on sustainable farm practices, has carefully evaluated agricultural efficiency. The best return on labor and resources uses human muscle to raise vegetable crops. Adding livestock to the equation demands a higher input of energy than is gained in output. Large-scale livestock husbandry offers even the illusion of benefit only when there is free (or subsidized) land available. Thus, we see rich ranchers in the United States who profit nicely from federal welfare, in the form of bargain-basement grazing fees.

In most poor regions of the world, land is precisely the problem. Due either to overcrowding or to unjust distribution of wealth (and the two usually go hand-in-hand), poverty means paucity of garden space. And providing more mouths to feed will not feed more people, it will feed fewer (this is not my opinion—it is simply a matter of thermodynamics).

It's the same reason that the much-heralded Green Revolution has had decidedly mixed results. The high-yielding strains of corn and wheat that were seen as a panacea for world hunger require enormous injections of water and fertilizer. If the starving masses had water and fertilizer (and, of course, land) they would not be starving in the first place.

The average American's diet, heavily based on meat-and-dairy consumption, requires twenty times the land area needed to feed a strict vegetarian. Beef consumption is skyrocketing in wealthy countries around the globe. The clear-cutting of forests for grazing land is not merely incidental to this voracity, it is intrinsic. Increasing the world's livestock burden will not make anyone better off—except the livestock merchant. The best gift of life we could possibly offer to malnourished Third Worlders would be to stop subsidizing Western beef production and McBurgerphilia exports. If meat prices reflected thermodynamic reality, the true resource costs would at least be apparent.

In a world economy in which the poorest people in the poorest countries starve while exporting food to the U.S., charity truly begins at home—on our own plates.

Jack (of beanstalk fame) was remarkably prescient in his business dealings. Give a woman some beans and a place to grow them, and she will feed a village. Give that woman a cow, and she will feed the cow.

Good things from the garden

Wouldn't it be nice if every book you owned and loved had pages as tough and durable as those in a Bible? The imported paper used in most Bibles is not only thin, but acid-free to boot, which means it might last hundreds of years without deteriorating.

Wouldn't it be nice if your favorite jeans and sneakers lasted twice as long?

Wouldn't it be nice if the brown grocery bags made of recycled paper didn't bust out at the bottom so easily?

Wouldn't it be nice if farmers didn't have to spray tons and tons of pesticides (the greater part of all pesticides used in this country) on cotton crops?

Wouldn't it be nice if your computer's case were completely recyclable?

Wouldn't it be nice if there were a healthy meat alternative that tasted better than tofu?

Wouldn't it be nice if there were an alternative to mega chip mills that are grinding our forests into paper-towel feedstock?

Wouldn't it be great if there were a single solution to all of those problems?

Well, there is! Bibles, tough jeans and sneakers, better quality recycled paper, insecticide-free farming, biodegradable computers and delicious, healthy protein are a few of the benefits of industrial-grade hemp. It is far past time to re-legalize hemp production in the United States, and join the growing number of hemp-exporting countries in the world. Hemp is not a cure-all for the pressing needs of industrial society, but it is clearly part of the answer.

At present, American Bibles, hemp clothing, hemp seed and oil, hemp paper and hundreds of other hemp-based products all depend on imports from France, Germany, Poland, Hungary, China—and, as of March 1, 1999, Canada has legalized the crop.

To hemp's many advocates, the story is a familiar one, but for the benefit of others, I will briefly recap. Hemp is the one of the oldest—and, arguably, most valuable plants known to agriculture. It has been a major fiber source for nearly ten thousand years; used for paper, rope and clothing. Hemp was an important crop in colonial America, and farmers even used it to pay their taxes. Both George Washington and Thomas Jefferson were major producers who exhorted their fellow citizens to grow hemp for the good of the young country. Early drafts of our Constitution were written on hemp paper, and hemp-seed cakes fed settlers and livestock alike.

By the end of the 19th century, the U.S. was a major hemp producer, and with the introduction of new technology for separating the long, strong fibers, we were poised to become the first high-tech hemp society. Headlines declared it to be the billion-dollar crop, Henry Ford produced an automobile almost entirely derived from hemp, and the Navy's demand for rope in World War I made the growing of hemp a patriotic duty.

Then, one man with a ton of money, a publishing empire and major investments in tree-pulp production decided to kill the burgeoning hemp industry. William Randolph Hearst used his newspaper monopoly to vilify hemp and twist public opinion. Joined by Andrew Mellon (who feared competition in his oil market) and Lammot Du Pont (whose empire was founded on petroleum-based chemistry), Hearst wielded money and influence to persuade Congress to make the plant illegal. The fear of Reefer Madness replaced environmental and agricultural sanity. We are all the losers.

Today's clearcuts, pulpwood plantations, chip mills, pervasive pesticide pollution, and even the failure of small family farms can, in large degree, be laid at the feet of three rich men—and one stupid congressional error.

In the meantime, hemp research has not stopped elsewhere, and the number of uses for the plant has grown explosively. Besides producing four times as much fiber per acre as trees (and better quality fiber, at that), hemp can be used to make paints and varnishes, medicines, renewable biomass fuel, snack food, biodegradable plastics and a wide range of fabrics.

Some people believe that they can find answers to all of life's questions in the Bible. If they are willing to include the paper underneath the print, I'd say it would be very hard to disagree.

"Where ignorant armies clash by night..."

We were down below the cliffs, jumping from rock to rock, watching gulls and gazing south along the Newfoundland coast toward the Tablelands, where stark, rusted, barren mountains tumble into the sea. Those mountains tell a lengthy tale about tectonic movement and the collision of continents over billions of years. They are naturally treeless because their bedrock is infertile, even slightly toxic: material that was shoved up from the earth's core when North America and Europe did The Bump in an impossibly distant age.

Fascinating stuff, this floating crust we call terra firma. It comes up from the depths as lava or is lifted by forces so powerful that solid stone acts like warm plastic: bending, folding, mutilating in rifts and layers and incursions. Elsewhere, it is falling back into the middle, drawn down into oceanic trenches as continents spread apart. The cliff wall behind me exhibits warped layers of slate, interspersed with crystal quartz and greenish malachite intrusions. No new rock here, only movement.

A little more accessible, in time scale at least, are the boulders recently sheared from the cliff. One must exercise caution walking below such escarpments—new material chunks off with each retreat of the sea. Between the rocks, ephemeral tide pools form a slow slide show, changing a little with every flow and ebb. Tiny shrimp, crabs, mussels and an occasional fish wiggle out an existence at the margin.

Across the inlet, I spot a moored boat canted slightly to one side, grounded until the incoming water floats it once again. The sight is familiar in Maritime Canada, as it is in any tidal basin or port around the world. A modest vessel needn't be moored in a deep channel if it is designed to sit comfortably on the strand.

Back in 1962, President John F. Kennedy famously remarked, "A rising tide lifts all boats." Not a surprising observation for a sailor to make, but it caught on, seen as an apt metaphor for a growing economy. However, Mr. Kennedy was wrong. That was very clear to me as I slid around on the seaweedy sea bed, pondering plate tectonics and barnacles, treeless slopes and fish.

The truth is that a rising tide lifts all boats *here*. But in order for the tide to rise in Rocky Harbor, it has to fall somewhere else. No new water, only movement. That is where Kennedy's metaphor fails, and why it continues to misinform the current economic debate. When used to support the argument that worldwide economic growth can lift the developing world out of poverty—without any need for sacrifice on the part of the rich—it conveniently begs the fundamental question: How can the tide be high everywhere at once?

Economic growth does not occur in a vacuum. The Western technocracies are rich because they appropriate seventy-five percent of the world's wealth, all of which is based on natural resources. The tide is high here because we make it low somewhere else.

Current, carefully reasoned scientific guesses suggest we now exceed the earth's natural resource production and carbon dioxide absorption limits by at least thirty percent. That is, we are living on our capital, not on interest from our ecologic accounts. Western resource use alone already outpaces sustainable levels, even if the poorest two-thirds of the world's people simply disappeared.

(We're not lifting their boats—we're punching holes in them.)

Efficiency gains are often touted as a way around such zero-sum accounting, but while potentially helpful, they are not a solution in and of themselves. The average auto in the U.S. is more efficient than thirty years ago (despite the popularity of gas-guzzling SUVs), but we drive many more miles and, consequently, use more fuel. Any real progress toward resource equity will require reduced demand from the rich.

A few hours later, the vessel across the harbor swings on it's mooring line, as a freshening westerly blows waves into a white froth against the black-slate palisades. All the boats in Rocky Harbor, Newfoundland, are on the rise—while, at Dover beach, perched on distant England's white-cliffed shore, the tide is running out.

•••

Note for the current edition: Ten years later the latest estimates suggest we are living forty percent above sustainability—we're moving backwards at the rate of one percent per year.

High hopes in Glen Canyon

Each of us carries an internal diorama, a series of illustrations from the flow of human enterprise that's led to here and now. These snapshots tend to capture iconic events—we whip out our cameras for birthdays and Christmas, or keep albums of babies and weddings. Our conscious awareness is low bandwidth—we can handle only a tiny slice of the whole shebang at any given moment—and we necessarily condense our knowledge to facilitate comprehension.

So we have Washington crossing the Delaware, the Alamo and D-day to symbolize wars, or driving a golden spike, the glow of Edison's bulb and one small step on the moon to capture technological change. In the more distant past, a slope-headed, skin-clad muscle-man with a stone hammer may represent a millennium, and a mounted barbarian can stand in for the clash of cultures over centuries. In recent history, we have Nixon's odd farewell, the demolition of the Berlin Wall, or a solitary figure facing a tank in Tiananmen Square to encapsulate much larger stories.

The most potent emblems of the current era are profoundly intertwined. First came the mushroom cloud at Hiroshima, announcing the end of innocence and the beginning of global awareness—which coalesced around the Apollo 10 photograph of the whole Earth. These two symbols, now shared and understood by the vast majority of our planetary population, form the bedrock of environmentalism: We have seen what we hold in common, and we know that we can destroy it.

It is time to add a third image to our global framework, a picture that demonstrates that we can save our heritage, too. It is time to move beyond the stopgap efforts of cleaning up spills, trading wetlands for development permits, scrubbing smokestacks and planting a few trees to replace the disappearing millions.

It is time to dismantle the Glen Canyon Dam.

If there is no more potent symbol of technological threat than the atomic bomb, there is no clearer demonstration of misguided technological hubris than a mega-dam. We strangled the Colorado River and created Lake Powell—with little understanding of what damage would ensue—simply because we could. Forty years poorer and wiser, we can now choose to undo our mistake. There could be no grander image to signal our new awareness than restoring the Grand Canyon.

Any dam sucks life from a river, but in arid regions, the damage is compounded. Evaporation and absorption claim one million acre feet of Lake Powell water per year—about eight percent of the Colorado River flow. That water, which once supported life from the Grand Canyon to the Gulf of California, is now unavailable for humans or wildlife, and the mighty Colorado no longer reaches the Pacific. In addition, the deep lake is chilly, and the 47-degree water exiting the turbines is too cold to support native aquatic species. The electric power produced by the Glen Canyon dam can be economically obtained from other sources—the region is ideal for both wind and photovoltaic power generation. Such replacement would double the inspiration value of this project, in one swoop restoring a wild river and embracing sustainable technology.

The Glen Canyon Institute is spearheading the campaign to free the Colorado River, and the Sierra Club has endorsed the plan. A congressional committee has been studying the proposal this year—a small victory in itself, given the current anti-environmental bias in Washington. Ecologists estimate that the plant and animal life along the banks of the river would recover within one year. The Grand Canyon, a land form so immense that an astronaut looking back from Mars could trace its course, will spring back to life. Egyptians enduring the calamitous effects of the Aswan High Dam will learn that they might yet save the Nile. The Chinese, determined to choke the Yellow River with the biggest dam ever, might even be convinced to step back before they, too, kill a precious artery.

The Bomb. The Whole Earth. The Canyon.

"To life!"

IV. The way you do the things you do

You come talking light, but you come walking dark,
The truth of your actions show the secrets of your heart,
We shall surely be known forever
by the tracks we leave.
~Carrie Newcomer
Tracks

In towns and cities across the country, people are
saying something is wrong with a world trading system
accountable to no one save the corporations that created
and control it. And they can't understand why
organizations like the WTO, the International Monetary
Fund and the World Bank have thousands of rules
protecting copyrights and patents and corporate rights,
but no rules protecting workers' and human rights
and the global environment.
~John Sweeney
President, AFL-CIO

The rules are not different here

Luckily for the rest of you, I'm the patient type. Otherwise, I'd be knocking some heads together, instead of making this tiny attempt at education.

"Forbear," I tell myself.

"They know not what they do."

The core problem emanates from confusion about "indoors" and "outdoors." A whole slew of you behave as if you didn't live here, on Big Blue, with the rest of us. You ignore the reality that the whole wide world is our living room, and living-room rules apply.

I spend a lot of time outdoors. I picnic. I camp. I hike. I paddle a canoe. I've been doing these things for most of my 48 years, and I learned *Rule One* before I escaped from grade school. *Rule One* belongs in every core curriculum: It is more important than math, language skills, social studies or art. *Rule One* should be chiseled into the marble keystone of every arch on every public building in the world. *Rule One* should be part of the oath of office.

Rule One Rules!

Rule One: Always leave a place cleaner than you find it.

There. That didn't hurt much, did it? It seems so simple, so practical, so fundamental, that it should have been tacked on to our genetic code before we dropped out of the trees. (Maybe it was, but it proved to be recessive. This could explain both my attitude and the "Random acts of kindness..." bumper-sticker crowd.)

Imagine how different the world could be, if *Rule One* were always and everywhere *Rule One*. What if every person leaving a grocery store plucked a single piece of trash from the ground and popped it in the can? (It's pretty obvious that, if everyone obeyed the rule, there wouldn't be trash for plucking, but scofflaws will doubtless persist. Violation of *Rule One* probably merits capital punishment.)

Nowhere is *Rule One* more flagrantly abused than in the countryside. Idiots may toss McWrappers and butts out their car windows in town, but wide open spaces seem to invite eyesore-ism, a nasty compulsion to dirty. If such behavior were limited to the criminal dolts who dispose of household garbage on road shoulders, we could at least infer a motive: saving on trash-collection fees. But, no, it is obviously the *lovers* of the outdoors who are trashing our habitat.

When I hike five miles into the mountains in a place inaccessible to vehicle traffic, I do it to enjoy the scenery, the wildlife, the fresh air and the exercise. I have to imagine that anyone who preceded me had similar motives. If my predecessor had a baby in tow, I can't help believing there was some intent to imbue the tyke with that selfsame appreciation for the wild.

So, why the diaper? Is a used diaper supposed to enhance my wilderness experience? Does it represent some sort of territorial claim, like an animal leaving its scent? Is it art?

(Of course, places accessible only on foot are a whole bunch cleaner than the places autos go to play—you don't haul used appliances into the outback. On the other hand, the current craze for 4x4 SUVs is extending the vehicular assault ever deeper into the woods.)

Speaking of diapers brings me to *Corollary One*, which addresses the most disgusting abuse of *Rule One:* Bury it.

You know what I mean. When nature calls, bury it. If you have even a small handful of neurons between your ears, you surely have a shovel in your trunk when you head out to picnic or camp. If you have only half a handful, or someone stole the hardware, use your heel to dig a little cat hole in the dirt. Use a stick. Use a rock. Use your hand if you have to, but bury it. And the t.p.

What is it with you people, hanging used t.p. in the bushes? Do you expect to re-use it, after a couple of good rain storms? Take my word on this one: Nobody else is going to use it. And nobody else wants to see it, either.

That's all for now: one rule; one corollary.

But next time, I'm gonna start knocking heads.

How you gonna keep 'em down in Belize after they've seen MTV?

The twenty million dollars Michael Jordan was paid to promote Nike shoes WAY exceeds the annual payroll of the plant that manufactures those sneakers. Like the colonial empires of the past, Nike extracts resources and labor from its colonies and turns a profit at home. Unlike those colonial empires, however, Nike tells the colonials all about it. Whereas a 17th-century East Indian laborer or Chinese coolie had only the sketchiest notion of the wealth of British monarchs, today's peasants have MTV.

MTV reaches more eyes and ears than any other information source in history. If knowledge is power, and if feedback loops produce turbulence, MTV is poised to become the wellspring of revolution in an acceleratingly unequal world. There are millions who would love to be in Michael Jordon's shoes, but at one-hundred-and-fifty bucks a pair, the fifteen-cent-an-hour workers who make them haven't got a shot at more than a shoestring.

Imagine, then, the impression America's dietary news must make in the far colonial corners of the world. While countless folks starve to death abroad, we test-market foods with no nutritional value whatsoever, in order to continue our satisfying gluttony without losing our swimsuit figures. Peasants are being driven off their ancestral lands to make way for export plantations; indigenous tribes are watching their forest homes fall to multinational axes; and alien mining poisons the fisheries that have fed villages practically forever—while we munch potato chips guaranteed to slide through our pipes without leaving a trace. "Let them eat Simplesse!" we cry.

At the same time, the dispossession of native populations encourages ecological devastation in the ensuing scramble for food and fuel.

All of which helps illustrate why economic justice is a linchpin of the struggle toward a sustainable world economy. Even if we are comfortable with the economic Grand Canyon that separates the have-lots from the have-nots (and the evidence is that, by and large, we are), we live in an MTV world. Our side of the divide is visible to others as never before. If simple morality doesn't motivate us, pipe bombs, plutonium and anthrax may provide an unsubtle nudge.

Perhaps the clearest expression of this idea is contained in *The Natural Step*, which originated in Sweden. Its founder, Karl-Henrik Robért, saw that while scientists did not agree on all ecological problems and solutions, there was near unanimity about the coming crisis. He cut through the quibbling—about how bad global warming might get, what the precise mechanism of ozone depletion might be, who deserved the blame for acid rain, and so forth—by putting together a set of agreed-upon principles. He circulated the ideas to all interested scientists in Sweden, and rewrote the plan 21 times to reach a final form in 1989. Now, the Swedish government—and many of the country's major industries —have adopted these rules. Published reports say it is moving the entire nation toward sustainability.

The root of Robért's theory is the cyclic principle, which says that there must be as much reconstruction of material as there is consumption. From that base concept, we get:

   I. Nature cannot withstand a systematic buildup of dispersed matter mined from the earth's crust (minerals, oil, etc.).

   II. Nature cannot withstand a systematic buildup of persistent compounds made by humans (e.g., PCBs).

   III.Nature cannot withstand a systematic deterioration of its capacity for renewal (e.g., harvesting fish faster than they can replenish, or converting fertile land to desert).

   IV. Therefore, if we want life to continue, we must:

       1. be efficient in our use of resources, and

       2. promote justice—because ignoring poverty will lead the poor, in the name of short-term survival, to destroy resources (e.g., the rain forests) that we all need for long-term survival. (Source: *Utne Reader*, February 1996, pp. 26-28.)

In 1994, eco-economist Paul Hawken signed on as president of the American Natural Step Group, which assembled a panel of scientific advisors to write a plan for the U.S. This fall, the Vision 2001 conference brought together industrialists and environmentalists in Lake Placid to explore *The Natural Step* as a path toward sustainability. In next to no time at all, the world will judge our progress.

After all, they've got their MTV.

Let it rain

There is less newsgathering going on today than any time in the past 40 years, but there's more news reporting than ever. Kind of weird, isn't it?

What we are seeing is less and less factual content and more and more opinion—like the commentary you are reading right now. Meanwhile, the number and diversity of information sources is exploding. People still put their pants on one leg at a time, but you can get that startling report in newsletter, newsprint, tabloid, magazine, radio, video, cable, satellite, on-line, pointcast or broadcast form. Your beeper can give you basketball scores while you sit at a football game watching hockey on your 4-inch color TV. The scrolled text that once appeared on TV screens only to announce imminent tornadoes is now a full-time alternative input on many cable channels. Multimedia rules!

Twenty-five years ago, I read a science-fiction story—the name of which escapes me—about a world in which Information Sickness had become epidemic. Peoples' brains were breaking down because of overload. As the data-bit stream accelerates, I think about that book and wonder if the epidemic is at hand. As a curious sidelight to this issue, I have spent more than six hours—in four public libraries in two states—and considerable time on the World Wide Web, without being able to track down that sci-fi tale. I can access mountains of facts, whole mountain ranges of supposedly vital information, but I can't even find the right haystack—let alone the needle that I know is there.

As a survival tactic, we cope with the data blizzard by focusing on a manageable handful of ideas—and ignoring the rest. What emerges is a picture of our own devising, which begins to resemble talking to oneself in the mirror. The Internet provides the current extreme case: There are millions of sources and relatively few editors. When a net surfer accesses only what she wants to hear, she creates a personal wave of information and misinformation and rides toward an individualized beach. There can't be a beach party at the end of the day, because everyone winds up on a different continent. Common ground is disappearing. More and more, we experience echoes of Paul Simon's lyric, "A man hears what he wants to hear and disregards the rest."

On the darker side, however, even the sources themselves are being tailored to fit. Suppose you wanted to know who invented the telephone. Writer Wayne Grytting observes, "If you looked it up in most versions of Microsoft's Encarta Encyclopedia, you would discover Alexander Graham Bell's name. But if you look it up in the Italian edition, you'd learn the inventor was Antonio Meucci. Similarily, the light bulb was "simultaneously" invented by Thomas Edison and Britain's Joseph Swan in the American edition, but Edison disappears in the British version." Such disparities may be harmless tips of the data-base hat to local pride, but larger blocks of history are being rewritten, as well. Revisionism (familiar to American students of the Civil War—or the War Between the States, if you live south of the Mason-Dixon) results in the disappearance of Kurdistan in a Middle Eastern edition. Encarta a fits facts to local sensibilities, and the information revolution becomes disinformation with the click of a mouse.

Walter Cronkite used to be the most trusted man in America. His news was *the* news—the audience believed he was objective. Today, we are more skeptical. We assume that everyone has an angle, and that purportedly objective reporting is merely pretense. We never considered reviewing Mr. Cronkite's investment portfolio. Today, we simply shrug when we learn that individual reporters or publishers have vested interests that color the news. Of course they do.

On the other hand, commentary takes sides and admits it. There is a level at which you can trust Rush Limbaugh, because you know where he stands. You may agree with me that he is usually way out in the ether, but at least his filter is obvious. You may think that my anti-growth, pro-population-control, anti-corporate, pro-solar-power biases are wrong-headed, but you can depend on me to stick to them. I believe absolutely that the only hope for human survival lies in a healthy ecosystem, that we are of nature and not apart from it. My prejudice colors my vision and my version of the news, and you know it.

As the storm of information rains down on us, commentary is a dry roof overhead—part of our coping strategy. The best we can hope to do is choose a few sources on the left and right—looking backward or forward, and deeply religious as well as humanist, technophile and Luddite—and then select our path. Without commentary to funnel the water into a handful of manageable streams, we would all be paddleless fools headed upcreek into the data-bit maelstrom.

•••

Note for the current edition: Gains and losses—News aggregator sites and responsible blogs are making editorial sense of the former chaos on the Web. Downside: corporate consolidation is putting fewer and fewer hands on the levers of mass media. The novel is Ted Mooney's *Easy Travel to Other Planets* (1981).

The crystal plummets

Raving tree huggers, myself included, sometimes claim we may be destroying planet Earth. Pie-eyed techno-idiots insist that everything will be peachy if we just dump environmental regulations and the Endangered Species Act, and let the free market rock and roll. Who is right? Is there any prayer that we can find common ground?

When I voice concern about the environment, I tend to believe that I support Life. But the truth is, my concern is for life like us. Bacteria are really neat little goobers, and we couldn't survive without them, but they did just fine without us for about ninety percent of the time since things began to wiggle on this planet. The urgency I feel about toxic waste or global warming involves preserving the current population of the planet. I have a fondness for oxygen-breathing, carbon-based life forms like dolphins and cats and gorillas and bats, hummingbirds and butterflies, tuna, termites, lizards— and people.

Well, some people, anyway.

When I factor people into the equation, it looks as though I might be speaking the same language as the movement that has adopted "wise use" as its slogan. The wise-users are the folks who want to permit mining, grazing and hunting in national parks, and who insist that old-growth forests are a renewable resource. They claim that global warming is an illusion, that there are no foreseeable limits to the human population of our planet, and that science will solve all of our problems by some time next week. They say the only useful measure of any policy is whether it is good for people, and they're fond of trotting out a few scientists to bolster their claims.

OK, let's go with that.

What? Me, a raving tree hugger, ready to accept the bottom line defined by earth rapers like Rush and Chainsaw Charlie? Have I been drinking to excess? My single caveat would be that we all must be willing to rely on real science, instead of rhetoric, to settle policy disputes. I am ready to concede any environmental debate on that basis. And by "real science," I mean the consensus of the majority of knowledgeable researchers in a given field.

Why do I say consensus? Shouldn't we demand scientific proof?

Nice idea, but science doesn't work that way. Outside of mathematics, where everything either adds up or it doesn't, proof is impossible. For example, if you release a crystal goblet ten feet above a brick patio, it will probably fall and shatter. Scientifically speaking, there is actually a tiny chance that it will bounce and land safely— and a much tinier chance that it won't even fall. But, based on our experience of gravity and bricks, most of us would agree that the crystal is history. In the same way, if the overwhelming majority of scientists agree about a particular issue, and one or a few disagree, the odds are very strong that the majority is correct.

Ready to be blinded by science?

In 1992, nearly sixteen hundred of the world's senior scientists, including more than half the living Nobel laureates—women and men from every discipline and every continent—signed The World's Scientists Warning to Humanity. More have signed it in the years since then.

In 1993, fifty-six of the world's scientific academies met for the first-ever world Science Summit and issued a collaborative statement.

Most of the world's scientists agree that, if the human race is to survive, we must reach zero population growth within the present generation. We must act now to shift from fossil fuels and nonrenewable resources to sustainable technologies. We must act now to reduce introduction of toxins and pollutants into the biosphere. We must act now to protect the biodiversity upon which all life depends.

Translation: The crystal goblet is headed toward the bricks.

There is nothing wrong with using human benefit as the measure of our policies, but short-term profit is a bad gage of success if it threatens long-term survival. If you are intent on amassing a fortune to leave to your heirs, you will also need some heirs to leave it to.

Are our current environmental-protection laws necessary?

Sorry, Charlie: We have barely begun.

Sprawl: urban and other

In the vale just below our ridge, a green tide has swept in this season, not necessarily a beneficent change. The green is a sprawling mat of chickweed or sandwort, introduced from who-knows-where, and indicating who-knows-what. The change has been dramatic and sudden, and such a rapid shift in an ecosystem suggests deeper, unseen transformation.

Weeds are more semiotic than botanical. A rose is a rose is a rose is a weed in a wheat field, and wheat a weed in a rose garden. Some weeds are sometimes welcome. We have been encouraging dandelions and winter cress for years, in hopes of getting a good mess of organic greens in the stew pot. Pigweed and poke are other congenial wild, edible interlopers.

On the other hand, some cultivars are pretty weedy. Mint is all but banished from the garden beds, since we have plenty for tea in the paths and margins. Comfrey has to be beaten back with steadfast regularity. In a broader context, imports such as purple loosestrife now crowd out native plants across the continent.

Working in the garden this spring, tending seedlings and digging weeds, I've been thinking about other growth, as well. The four-lane furies are blasting their way through a mountain pass this year, extending unwanted urban madness toward our valley. Over the past decade, Asheville's Chamber of Commerce has gone far out of its way to flog the town, and buyers are winging in like crows to sprouted corn.

Like most other cities, Asheville is eagerly courting new businesses, and state government stands ready to fund research into likely sites for new industry in the region. Somehow, city planners have convinced themselves that the only way to make a city better is through growth—and, additionally, that the best tonic for growth is new blood.

I think we need a little paradigm shift here, and perhaps a bit of redefinition. The buzz is all about sustainability, these days, which is generally perverted into sustainable growth. But city planners are too far from the farm to understand what real sustainability is all about. Perhaps they should spend less time at their desks and more time in the garden.

Farmers tend to be conservative about new crop varieties. They learn what works in their soil and in their climate zone and try to repeat success. Any experiments with novel seed stock are usually incremental and tentative. Such circumspection pays off handsomely in a reliable food supply for the rest of us. Betting the whole farm on a loser could be catastrophic—to farmer and consumer alike.

Furthermore, plant genetics plays a part in a grower's success. By selecting seed from the healthiest, most-productive plants, one can develop varieties well adapted to local conditions. Adopting native weeds is another way to take advantage of a good genetic/climatic fit. Winter cress, known hereabouts as cressy or creasey greens, is a wild plant that's now widely cultivated.

The farm model works for cities and regions aiming for sustainability, as well. Building on past success with businesses that have thrived over time, with institutions that are strong in their years, with people who have been around long enough to see what works, is the natural path to long-term stability. New businesses should be regarded as untested weeds—suspect until proven otherwise, and definitely not to be blindly encouraged. Those suited to local conditions will take root and flourish on their own. Those unsuited don't deserve space in the garden.

Big businesses circling the globe seeking sweet deals are particularly to be shunned. Like those flocks of crows settling on the corn rows to pluck tender sprouts, multinationals are out for easy pickins and apt to fly off south tomorrow. Cultivating deals with Kudzu International is a fast track to calamitous crop losses.

Come to think of it, a city interested in healthy growth might do well to invest in an economic scarecrow, stuffed with impact fees, excise taxes and difficult permitting regs. As for the weedy franchises, a little cultivation between the rows of existing business should be enough to keep newbies cut down to size.

Goin' down to Yasgur's farm

There is no more enduring decision we make in our lives than how we choose to use the land we control. Even if your parcel is only a quarter-acre city lot, you can make a four-hundred-year decision by cutting down an old oak tree in the yard. Larger holdings invite longer impact. Some of the world's deserts were apparently created by human error. Oops—there goes the neighborhood!

That potential for good or ill obviously makes our collective choices critical—and contentious. Ever since we white folks stole this continent, we have embraced legal protection of property rights, which runs head-on into the need to provide for our common future. Back when the land seemed endless and our population was small, there wasn't much incentive for self-control. After cattle and sheep ate everything green, the herds were driven farther west. Loggers followed.

Now, we're getting crowded, and the choices we make will quite literally determine whether Americans starve in the next century. The farm land that feeds us is disappearing. The problem is both vertical and horizontal. Failure to solve both equations will invoke terribly painful consequences.

The vertical disappearance involves topsoil loss. This is a purely agricultural problem, and no one is more aware of the causes and cures than farmers. The nutrient-rich dirt that underlies all food production is washing down our rivers about one hundred times faster than nature can create new soil. There are solutions, but they will be expensive and slow. Simply rotating land out of production is an effective remedial method, but it requires expensive surplus acreage.

That leads to the horizontal problem: the growth of cities and suburbs. A farmer who is able to stop erosion may still face unbearable economic pressure to sell. Once arable land turns into subdivisions and shopping malls, the growing of food on it is over. Period. Plowing up pavement is not remotely feasible, on a meaningful scale.

One radio listener told me that the real villain in urban sprawl is the lowly septic tank, which makes widely dispersed housing affordable. Sharp restrictions in septic permits would let sewer accessibility centralize growth patterns. That seems simple enough, but is probably politically impossible. The old standoff between property rights and public good rears its ugly head.

Perhaps a more workable approach would be to offer full tax exemption to farmers willing to lock their land into nondevelopment. In exchange for rezoning their property as permanent farm land, farmers would pay no property taxes. We now tax agricultural land at a reduced valuation, but this total exemption would actively discourage subdivision. We already extend this benefit to churches and other nonprofit groups. Offering it to the stewards of our land is at least as practical as helping out the stewards of our souls.

This option is already being explored, in a small way, by nonprofit land trusts. They buy farmers' land, while granting them the right to farm it in perpetuity—saving the family's farming, if not the family farm.

European countries faced such choices long ago, in a landscape that still bears the scars of Rome's imperial decisions. Continental life has been crowded for centuries, and farm land consequently more precious than here in the New World. In England, you cannot cut down a four-hundred-year-old tree—or even a hedge in your yard—without specific permission from the government. And modern forestry began as a German response to deforestation. But Europe had at least two safety valves that we will not: the Black Death and colonialism. The demise of every second person in the 1300s was a great benefit to the survivors, at a time when the food supply was problematic. This was followed by massive emigration to new colonies.

Today, there is no frontier that can absorb our burgeoning population, and modern medicine is likely to combat the sort of population relief seen in 14th-century Europe. Ebola, anthrax and AIDS are not nice ways to depopulate. But neither is starvation. Not choosing to save farm land now will force massive hardship—within our children's lifetimes.

When our farms grow Wal-Marts and suburban mini-estates, instead of food, we are all in deep trouble. Developers may say, "Let them eat Moon-Pies!" But we can say, "Stop!"

•••

Note for the current edition: We seem to be making some progress on setting aside conservation easements here in Buncombe County and across the country. We can only hope that the practice accelerates quickly. Time is running out.

All I need is the air that I breathe

Recently, Professor Harvard Ayers of Appalachian State University headed a study of northern hardwood forests in the Southern Appalachians. He reports that thousands of acres of beech, maple and yellow birch are dying and not growing back. Nor is the phenomenon limited to that region.

I have lately traveled most of the length of the nation's eastern mountain chain, and the failure is pandemic. From New Hampshire and Vermont through the Berkshires and Adirondacks, down along the Shenandoah Valley and into the Virginias and Carolinas, the failure is evident. Reports from around the world concur: Arizona's saguaros, western Douglas fir, Florida's palms and Canadian spruce are dying, as are European and Asian trees.

But don't take my word for it—look for yourself.

Deciduous trees impacted by air pollution die first at the tips. Look for bare branches there. In the winter, note that upper branches don't have as many twigs. In the spring, tops don't leaf out. Leaves become smaller each season, and affected trees tend to shed green ones before autumn.

Failing evergreens look yellowed or brown instead of deep green. They produce an overabundance of cones, in a last effort at genetic survival.

All of these effects are most noticeable at higher elevations, and on slopes with western or southern exposures that receive prevailing winds. But the problem is moving downslope quickly. The effects Ayers found at the four-thousand-foot level on Mount Rogers are visible (though less severe) where I live, at three thousand feet in the Swannanoas.

We can talk about fifty things to do to save the earth until we are blue in the face—literally. We need five hundred things. Whatever you are doing now to help, assume it is not enough. Drive fewer, slower miles. Work at home, or lobby your employer to adopt four ten-hour days, instead of five eights. That alone can cut commuting miles by twenty percent. Better yet, ride your bicycle, or walk. Turn down the thermostat. Use twenty-five percent less electricity. Turn off the TV. Turn off the water heater every other day. Become a vegetarian. Use everything until it is worn out.

A thoughtful society confronted with an airborne environmental catastrophe would impose a carbon tax, ration electricity, drop speed limits to 45 mph, ban beef production and car racing, discourage reproduction, fund solar power and stop subsidizing oil and coal. But, absent real campaign-finance reform, big money controls Congress, and the fossil-fuel industries are the big boys on the block.

Last year, however, B.P. and Shell decided to quit supporting the disinformation campaign, saying that their futures lay in conservation and renewable energy. We may get help from other unlikely quarters, too. Insurance companies report that severe-weather-related damage claims have climbed five-fold in the past two decades. This is a direct result of the climatological change we are creating. But insurance companies cannot afford the bigger, more powerful hurricanes, torrential rains interspersed with extended drought, and other weather anomalies that lie ahead, and so may be allies in the drive toward a sustainable economy.

This underscores one of the big lies that is often repeated by conservative economists and ideologues: that radical change will wreck our economy, and that it will be cheaper to fix problems in the future than to change course now.

Radical rapid change will definitely hurt some businesses, but it will be an era of limitless possibilities for others. Failure to change now, and quickly, will bring unfathomable catastrophe. In a warming world, rising sea levels will displace millions of people, long droughts will bring famine, tropical diseases will move into temperate zones, and violent storms will gain in frequency and strength. These symptoms are already upon us. The Antarctic ice cap is cracking, Alaskan tundra is melting, encephalitis has erupted in Florida, and Hugo and Andrew are harbingers of more to come.

Though political pressure is imperative, we can't afford to wait for government action. Environmental law is one of the biggest political success stories in this era, but legal change alone is not enough—and not fast enough. President Clinton's recent proposal to return to 1990 pollution levels by 2012 is a case in point. It will be too little and too late. A U.N. panel of twenty-five hundred scientists believes we need to drop 60 percent below 1990 levels—within a decade—to beat the heat.

It's up to us.

•••

Note for the current edition: This was pre-Katrina, before the Northwest Passage became ice-free in summer for the first time in millennia—back when we had winters here in Western North Carolina. And Clinton's weak-kneed effort was knee-capped by Bush. So it goes.

Winnowing, winnowing

While addressing a college seminar recently, I stumbled on an idea that seems worth exploring. There I was, blabbing away about sustainability and, whaddya know, something came out of my mouth that made me think.

Where did that come from? Did I say that?

But maybe I should backtrack a little. I was discussing the notion that, in order to move from our currently failing life-support system into some sort of mode that would work over the long term, we need to make numerous—and fairly drastic—changes.

Agriculture has created devastation since its inception. Once we humans broke out of the naturally occurring food chain and started to plant, plow, fertilize and irrigate, we began to wreak havoc. From the Fertile Crescent in Mesopotamia, where "civilization" began, we have marched around the world creating deserts, dust bowls and deforestation. On every continent, we have mined the topsoil—an irreplaceable resource, on any meaningful time scale. We have diverted more than half of the liquid fresh water on earth to serve human ends. Our pesticides have inundated the web of life, and hormone-mimetic chemicals are causing developmental failure and mutation worldwide.

In the past, there was always someplace else to go, but now, we have filled up the planet. Agriculture expanded for millennia, but in this generation, we have hit the wall. Arable land—that is, acreage usable for growing food crops—is decreasing. The modern agricultural solution has been to increase the energy input, to force more production from fewer acres. But that, too, seems to be reaching the limits imposed by photosynthesis and soil chemistry. No matter how much fertilizer we dump on a field, and no matter how carefully we time planting, cultivation and irrigation, and regardless of pest controls, we seem to be bumping our heads on a natural ceiling. And topsoil loss is on the rise.

So, the obvious course is to search for alternatives that will work over a longer term. In my discourse, I observed that the only model we have for a sustainable human culture is the pre-agricultural gatherer/hunter lifestyle, which lasted for about thirty-five thousand generations. No matter how you measure success, that should qualify for "long-term." Back then, there were four or five million of us.

This bit of history led to the question in question:

Could the modern American lifestyle prove to be sustainable for a world population that small? If all 5 million of us lived in technological luxury, could we make that journey last? Could the biosphere swallow the insult of such levels of pollution, over time?

It seems to me that a computer model could be designed (much like Bucky Fuller's World Game, or the atmospheric models used to explore global climate change) to estimate how many people would last how long if everyone lived our modern lifestyle—with all of our comforts, indulgences, waste production and pollution.

I suspect that a population of 5 million might do pretty well over a fairly long haul. But it's quite obvious that today's 6 billion humans cannot possibly achieve universal modernity, let alone sustain it—the waste heat from combustion and friction alone would cook everyone in a heartbeat. So the answer we need to discover lies in a domain bounded by two quantities. The first would be a plot based on our current population, with an estimate of how much we would each need to give up to achieve environmental stability. The other would be a plot based on America's current lifestyle, with an estimate of how many people we would have to eliminate in order for everyone left to be able to live as we do, happily ever after. Such an exercise would describe very vividly the horns of our dilemma.

At the same time, it would neatly illustrate thoroughly practical options. We might choose our present (and growing) population, with a life-style/consumption level somewhere around that of today's more advanced Third World nations; or we might opt for a world population that's closer to that of present day Phoenix, with everyone living like Bill Gates; or maybe some compromise, in between.

Then we can begin to decide who or what to get rid of, and who or what we really want to keep. Global agreement on such a target for sustainability may seem like a pretty tall order, but it will take tall answers to get us through the raging torrent of growth we now face. We are already way past knee deep.

(Note: Since writing this essay, I have been introduced to the *Ecological Footprint* concept, intro- duced in a 1996 book by Mathis Wackernagel & William Rees. Their calculations suggest that the earth can sustainably support considerably less than two billion people in the style to which Americans have become accustomed.)

•••

Note for the current edition: The bleakest current news I have read as of this writing in January, 2008, is that the U.S. is in the midst of a baby-boom. When will we learn?

The killing fields

A friend and I were reminiscing about lawns the other day.

Ah, the lawns of youth! Badminton and touch football. Croquet and cartwheels. Dandelions and clover.

Do those last two nouns sound particularly old-fashioned and quaint? They should, at least to anyone who pays attention to modern turf-management practices. Weed-free is the ticket these days, and chemical warfare is all the rage.

Looking around the garden section of any big department store, you have to wonder whether the real goal of American gardeners is growing things or killing things. In springtime, you literally have to "look around"—there are stacked pallets of poison climbing halfway to the ceiling, with displays near the checkout lines to encourage impulse buying. (If Saddam had simply opened a Wal-Mart in Baghdad, he could have stored his [nonexistent] secret weapons in plain sight, and no weapons inspector on earth would have thought twice about it.)

A close friend of mine who's in the lawn-care business reports that his customers expect him to use broadleaf weed killer five times during the season. Though he isn't particularly keen on it, he says he has to do it to be competitive. Asked if he isn't concerned about his own frequent exposure to toxic concoctions, he replies that he follows the label warnings, and that the manufacturers claim the stuff is safe.

Oh?

I don't mean to suggest that my buddy is gullible, or that the general public is a group of fools. If suburban homeowners routinely keeled over and expired after spreading Weed-n-Feed, their neighbors would presumably exercise caution in their own defoliation efforts. And it would be hard to find a reliable yard service, if turf surfers were dying in droves.

But, to begin with the obvious, herbicides are very unsafe for herbs—and all of the other targeted broadleaf species. Flowering plants—including dandelions and clover—are the food source for bees and butterflies, flies and moths. Those, in turn, represent lunch for spiders and birds and bats. Many of the insects and some of the birds and bats are pollinators—species that are fundamental to plant reproduction. That includes such incidentals as apples, wheat, okra and string beans.

So a chemical assault may not cause the fellow spraying to toss his cookies, but it could end with him losing his lunch.

Pollinator populations are collapsing, worldwide. Some farming has already been seriously impacted by this catastrophe, and numerous plant species are experiencing reproductive failure. We're talking whole food chains here, folks—whole ecosystems.

I am aware that this sounds somewhat alarmist, but if you bother to look a little further, it gets worse. We are altering the chemistry of our lovely blue planet in extremely dangerous ways. Our entire hydrologic system is permeated with non-natural chemicals: lakes, rivers, oceans—the works. The chemical soup we think of as clean drinking water increasingly contains hormone-mimetic and hormone-disrupting compounds that impact reproduction and cell division, even in minute quantities.

Not surprisingly (because of their close association with water), among the first to feel the impact have been fish, marine mammals and sea birds. Scientists are reporting birth defects, tumors and sexual debilitation in populations worldwide.

Among the primary causes of this complex biochemical disaster are pesticides that are legal and considered "safe when used as directed."

Obviously, lawn care is not the only source of these ubiquitous toxins, but it is an entirely unnecessary one. There is nothing inherently more attractive about a lawn without dandelions than one with dandelions. Consumers have been sold an idiotic AstroTurf image through decades of advertising by chemical companies, whose bottom line dictates their ethical relationship to the earth. ("Ethical" may be a bit of a stretch, here.)

Thinking back to my childhood, I remember picking ripened dandelion heads covered with fuzzy parachutes, making a wish—and blowing with all my might. I guess the idea was that a wish could come true if it was scattered on the wind.

What do people wish for when they spray Round-Up?

The change is gonna do me good

Each of us functions within sets of nested assumptions that direct both our actions and our perceptions of actions, personally and collectively.

Some physical assumptions, based on experience, are useful—we don't start from scratch each morning: Our feet will meet a floor as we tumble out of bed, the coffee maker will work the way it did yesterday, the clock on the wall is still in synch with the clock in the office, or at school. But some other physical assumptions, also based on perceived experience, can be flat wrong: Geocentrism comes to mind. (False assumptions are always easier to see in retrospect.) Still others, which we know to be wrong, continue to appear correct within certain contexts: Newtonian physics offers a good-enough estimate for everyday affairs, even if Einstein shot it full of (cosmo)logical holes.

I tender such physical examples to offer a metaphorical grip on the change that's needed to create a sustainable future. An enduring technological society will necessarily live within its local energy income, whether one defines "local" as bioregional or planetary. Today's technocracies run on fossil fuel—a savings account that is beginning to wear a little thin. Future success will require a change of consciousness as profound as the Einsteinian overthrow of Newton's apple cart.

A sustainable economy will be no-growth. The earth's biomass (the sum of all living matter) has remained approximately constant since the last ice age. Within the zero-sum economy of biology, more cattle means fewer trees, people replace grizzlies or antelope, and so forth. The emergent culture must be steady-state, instead of expanding.

Proprietary ownership of resources will have to go. Every resource decision impacts every living thing within the biosphere. The concept of private property at the disposal of an individual owner fails to address the stake-holding of others in the ecosystem.

A corollary will be that proprietary ownership of invention will disappear. The collective genius of our species has created a myriad of solutions to the problems we face. Some have been life-enhancing, others have proved literal dead ends—nuclear weapons and nerve gas being paradigmatic cases in point. And, although we have drawn fine legal lines that call one idea "mine" and another "yours," no idea exists in a vacuum. We have all contributed.

Individual ownership of resources and inventions is a recent historical development. The only model we have observed of a successfully sustainable human culture is the pre-agricultural gatherer/hunter lifestyle which lasted for about thirty-five thousand generations. The handful of similar cultures that survive still practice ownership in common and resource management for the benefit of all.

(This is not to suggest that gathering/hunting is now a viable option, but it does demonstrate that such all-for-one and one-for-all Three Musketeerism works.)

Coupled with this renewed sense of the commons, the private lending of money at interest will necessarily end. Such banking inexorably tends to concentrate ownership and control. Two hundred years into the American experiment, the conjunction of proprietary ownership and banking has resulted in one person, Bill Gates, controlling more wealth than the poorest 40 percent of the world's population. Whether such a kingpin is a saint or the devil incarnate, this concentration of wealth and power inevitably impoverishes and disempowers the mass of humanity.

On these matters, Karl Marx was every bit as wrong as Adam Smith. The future belongs to cooperative individualism, in which we control our own lives but not one another's—like a wolf pack, pod of whales or flock of birds composed of self-reliant units that tend to themselves and their young.

How can we share resources and still find motivation? How can communal benefit supplant personal gain and yet retain individual autonomy? One model is the human body. All of our cells and organs are interdependent, yet the liver manages to be different from the stomach—without no-fly zones and trade wars. To adapt Ben Franklin's phrase, our organs must all hang together—otherwise, we fall apart.

Einstein bent Newtonian space to offer a glimpse of a greater Universe than we had ever before imagined. Our task today is to bend our thoughts, to question assumptions, to dare to challenge what is held to be true and dear.

Upon this great work hangs our survival.

V. Not the economy, stupid

*Perhaps it has never been more necessary than now,
to say what the myths say: that a well-ordered
humanism does not begin with itself,
but puts things back in their place.
It puts the world before life, life before man, and
the respect of others before love of self.
This is the lesson that the people we call 'savages'
teaches us: a lesson of modesty, decency and discretion
in the face of a world that preceded our species
and will survive it.*
-Claude Lévi-Strauss
Psychology Today, May 1972

Live complexly, that others may...

Book blurb: "when ... living simply and wholly seems beyond our reach ..."

T-shirt: "Chop wood, carry water."

Bumper sticker: "Live simply, that others may simply live."

Ah, yes. Let's reach back and pick up the thread that we lost somewhere between the World Wars—the good life we savored before everything turned complicated. There's just too much information in this Information Age!

The idea is appealing—that one can embrace simplicity in a more natural setting, strip away modern busy-ness, and somehow reduce the inputs into one's aching cranium.

The idea is wrong.

Chopping wood and carrying water are far more complex experiences than setting a thermostat, turning on the faucet and paying utility bills. Furthermore, it's precisely that complexity that gives such utilitarian efforts their appeal. Not only do you have to think more about living when you do it yourself, you experience life at a wider bandwidth. All of your senses are engaged.

This inversion of popular wisdom became clear to me while considering my outhouse. Among all of the accouterments of my alternative lifestyle, it's the composting toilet that most interests (and/or repels) visitors. It suddenly struck me that a composter embodies a lot more information than most people customarily deal with.

The modern bathroom is hermetic. While using it, one contemplates square tiles, pastel towels, tasteful wallpaper and, perhaps, a faint chemical odor, or the hum of a ventilation fan. The experience is repetitive and banal, completely cut off from the living earth. The circle is broken.

My composter, having no door, provides a montane panorama of forested ridges and valleys, clouds gathering above the tallest peak and spilling into the gorge, snow flurries swirling, pileated woodpeckers swooping and laughing, and the rich odor of organic decay—a smell more or less trenchant in direct correlation to recent ambient air temperature. The experience is constantly varied and forces direct connection between one's physicality and the planet underfoot. The loop is complete.

The reason modern life is often reduced to a sensual desert is that one of civilization's primary goals is reducing, not increasing, information. The less one needs to know in order to survive, the more conscious attention can be directed toward social interaction. "Free" time emerges—and, thus, the demand for entertainment. As Tor Nørretranders observed in his landmark work, *The User Illusion*, the shortcoming of modern communication and entertainment is that they occur largely within the narrow bandwidth of conscious attention. Unfortunately, our consciousness processes only fifteen to thirty bits of information per second, whereas our brains handle many millions. That means that, while we are chuckling our way through a sit-com, our brains are bored silly.

The "simple" life is remarkably free of free time, but deliciously full of neural stimulation.

Bread-making is far more interesting than buying a loaf. And, to add to the complication, one can grow the wheat, grind it and culture sourdough before commencing with the mixing, kneading, raising and baking. Homemade bread is high bandwidth; Wonderbread is not.

The same can be said for gardening vs. shopping for frozen veggies. Participating in nutrient cycles, mulching to battle drought, weeding in August heat, and racing to gather peppers before a killing frost are viscerally engaging. Homegrown food is high bandwidth; frozen pizza is not. (Microwave meals are real food with most of the information removed.)

Even the Zen twins, chopping and carrying, are decidedly unsimple. How much wood do you need to prevent frostbite in an average winter? In an extreme one? Is it dry or green? Are there more Btus in locust or maple or oak or hickory? How many hours of splitting effort will return to humus if one cuts too much? And then there's kindling, matches, ashes and, finally, blackberries.

(Blackberries and other cane fruits quickly crowd into the sunlight where a tree has been felled.) While you contemplate the utter simplicity of a thermostat, note that I still have not mentioned the pungent smell of freshly cut and split wood, the gratifying snap/crack of a well-placed maul stroke, the satisfying ache in shoulders and back after an afternoon in the wood lot, the stove dance performed by chilled bodies basking front and back by the wood burner, or the contemplative effect of firelight on hand-hewn beams.

Ah, sweet complexity at last!

One, two, three, four, look at the score

Have you ever labored to put together a big jigsaw puzzle, only to confront the disappointing discovery that pieces were missing? You invested all that time and wound up with an incomplete picture. If you lacked the very concept that pieces could be missing, and didn't look at the photo on the box, you might even think the image in front of you was complete as intended. And if, instead of a picture, it was an economic theory you were piecing together, you might believe your equations were correct, even if important numbers were missing.

Capitalism, which is the big jigsaw puzzle of our economic life, is exactly that kind of flawed theory. Now a few economists have pushed their chairs back from the table, noticed missing pieces on the floor, and snapped the figures into place. They call the finished picture Natural Capitalism.

Capitalism has always been a pretty good theory. It seems only logical that people will act in their own best interest. The lowest prices on the best goods and services will attract customers. Efficient businesses will win out, because they make the best use of capital and deliver what the people want. Given a level playing field, everyone can play the game and win.

The only monkey-wrench in the works has been that we never looked very closely at how we were keeping score. False assumptions in our accounting system meant that the playing field was never level, after all. Natural Capitalism reassesses the basic facts—and, suddenly, the scoreboard looks very different.

The biggest error has been in our valuation of natural resources. We have assumed that their only real cost has been that of extraction. For example, under the old system, a tree has no value until it is cut down. Then the value increases when it is transported, sawed, milled and used for furniture, paper or homes. Because we didn't understand the real worth of a standing tree, we skewed the whole system toward inefficiency and destruction. The same is true for other raw materials—there is a built-in assumption that the natural world is an unlimited source of freebies.

At the same time, we assumed that the only cost of waste disposal was in hauling and burial. We placed very little value on garbage and didn't wonder what happened to all of the junk we dumped into river basins, wetlands or oceans. Air and water pollution were not considered negatives: They cost nothing, unless we cleaned them up. And, if and when we did, that cost was treated as a plus on the books.

This old scorekeeping system is called the Gross Domestic Product, which is the total dollar value of all goods and services sold in the country: the wages paid, the widgets produced, the professionals consulted, the booze sold and the 12-step programs funded, the buildings built and rebuilt after a bomb blast or tornado —everything that can be measured in cash, even the cost of government. When the GDP rises, the experts in Washington tell us that life is getting better.

The bizarreness of the GDP lies in the way all expenditures register as pluses. Cancer treatment, divorce proceedings, disaster relief, Prozac prescriptions and extra police protection in crime-ridden cities are every bit as good for the economy as growing food or building homes. The GDP completely ignores the effect of any particular spending.

The new view provided by Natural Capitalism suggests that we should place real value on the services provided by healthy ecosystems. The clean water and air created by a healthy forest are far more valuable than the wood products we derive from trees. When an economic value is assigned to fertile topsoil, productive fisheries and other natural resources that we formerly regarded as free, we can begin to see the real costs and benefits in our consumer choices.

Natural Capitalism encourages conservation. It favors more labor and less waste (recycling, for instance, creates more jobs than does a landfill). It evaluates products in terms of their overall impact, weighing effects in terms of benefit or harm, instead of simple dollar values.

The promise of Natural Capitalism is that everyone can benefit. In fact, the numbers suggest that businesses which ignore the new paradigm will fail in this increasingly crowded world, where people are common and resources dear. For environmentalists, the new view is cheering, which should be no surprise: The new capitalism is completely natural.

How do you like them apples?

Have you ever hiked along a hedgerow or followed an old stone wall and stumbled on an ancient apple tree, still bearing fruit after years of neglect? Have you whittled away the suspicious blemishes and brown spots with your pocketknife and tasted the sharp, winey sweetness? Have you tucked one in your backpack for later enjoyment while you wondered who planted the tree, and when?

Old fruit trees link us to the past. They demonstrate the long, slow sweep of human knowledge that sustains us—and, at the same time, the thinness of the thread by which we hang.

A friend of mine once observed that capitalists don't plant fruit trees. That may be too strong a statement, but surely, a pure capitalist would not experiment with apple culture. To commit land and labor and time to a speculative orchard requires curiosity and commitment and concern for the future that doesn't jibe with short-term profits. Even planting one's land with an old-reliable variety demands belief in long cycles of investment and benefit.

Once, while biting into a wild apple—or, rather, an apple gone wild—I imagined two orchardists meeting over the same stone wall, a century ago. The first offered the other a ripe, red fruit. The second polished it on his shirt front and took a bite. "Tasty," he allowed. "What is it?"

"They call it Jonathan. My cousin gave me seeds fifteen years ago; the trees work this ground real good. You should try it."

The first fellow tossed the core; a chipmunk toted it to the top of the wall, where he finished it off. The seeds fell between the stones.

Then I pictured the same two men meeting there fifteen years later, in the shade of a young apple tree. The second man held up two apples. "I planted a Jonathan; good growth. But try this Northern Spy—I think it's better."

Obviously, even simple exchanges of horticultural ideas and varieties can take generations. All of the standard cultivars of fruits that we eat today are the product of this long process of sorting and planting and thinking and rethinking. Whether you prefer big, shiny, tasteless apples with an extended shelf life, or the sharp bite of a Winesap, you partake of history. Even the dwarf and semi-dwarf varieties developed fairly recently demand years to prove their worth, and good trees will provide crops for decades, if not centuries.

At the same time, the viability of tough, long-lived trees like apples depends entirely on consistent and very local conditions. An orchardist who lives up the valley from me planted a proven local variety of tree on a likely stretch of his land, only to discover that he had made a mismatch. He finally abandoned his original site and planted again on a different slope, with somewhat different soil and drainage. This time, he was successful.

And when we toss factors like global climate change into the equation, it's easy to see that we hang from a very skinny lifeline. If a quarter of a mile's distance can make or break my neighbor's efforts, what will happen if temperature zones move forty miles north, or rain patterns and frost dates shift? Assuming that land is available, a bean crop can be planted successively farther upslope, or north. An old apple tree can't be moved, and a young one won't produce for years. A late frost can wipe out one year's fruit crop completely. What if late frosts come every year?

It's easy to be blasé about our food supply, with apples and oranges and pears and grapes piled high in grocery displays, year round. But it is something of a miracle that we enjoy such abundance, and miracles should never be taken for granted.

Sir Isaac Newton, so the story goes, based a lifetime of paradigm-shattering mathematical thought on the fall of an apple to earth. Consider the many lifetimes invested in raising apples to the sky, on branches that reach across a hundred years to place the fruits of some long-dead stranger's skill and foresight into your waiting hand: a profound communion, partaking of the sweat and blood of a hundred generations.

No wonder those apples taste like fine wine.

Remember, buy here now

Last week, I stopped in at a tropical-fish store to ask the owner two questions. Where do your fish come from? How are they collected?

My curiosity had been roused by reading about the devastating effect of fish collection on South Pacific reef systems. Unscrupulous collectors use poison and dynamite to simplify their enterprise, then sell the survivors. (Scrupulous sorts are, of course, also engaged in the forcible imprisonment of creatures for profit—raising a more fundamental question which will not comfortably fit in the present essay.) I wondered how the story played out on the retail end.

The unsurprising—and unsatisfactory—answer is that there are no guarantees. Marine tropical fish arrive with a certificate purporting to verify that they were ethically collected. But the person who fills out that form is a middleman, who may or may not know the actual collector or her methods. We get the semblance of honest self-regulation, but it's impossible to be sure.

This leads to a much broader inquiry: In a global economy, is it possible to be a responsible consumer?

I dropped by a local futon showroom—an outfit with a hard-sought reputation for environmental responsibility. The most attractive frame on display was made of plantation-raised mahogany. Hmmm. The salesman pointed out that wide sections had been glued up from narrow strips, because the farmed trees are younger and smaller than old growth from tropical rain forests. That *seems* convincing.

Then again, the oil-company ads touting great commitment to environmental protection seem pretty convincing, as well—they just happen to omit the stuff about pouring millions of dollars into fake grassroots efforts to repeal clean-air and -water regulations. I know, I know ... it's only a one-page ad, and they ran out of space. But you see the problem.

The upshot of such uncertainty is the growing movement toward radical localism. If you want to know beyond doubt that the organic carrot in your cake fits your definition of organic, grow it yourself. Any source of carrots beyond your back yard involves trust, and if late-20th-century merchandising has taught us one overriding lesson, it is that trust is subject to malevolent abuse. When supply lines stretch out around the globe, it is simply impossible to be sure.

Instead of crossing fingers and hoping for the best, the radical localist chooses new priorities. *In Act Now, Apologize Later*, Sierra Club President Adam Werbach sets out the radical-localism pact:

I will do my best to:
1. Buy products produced locally, products made with local ingredients and local labor.
2. Demand that outside corporations respect local culture and incorporate local products into their product base.
3. Know my community, both human and wild.

Here is the front line in the battle against Wal-Martization, against tax-funded, corporate-welfare schemes to lure multinational business development, and against the export of jobs. The radical localist isn't fooled by smiley faces and low prices that help destroy downtown businesses while funneling money into distant banks.

It's pie-simple to join the growing ranks of thoughtful consumers who understand that dollars are votes, and that those votes shape the places we live. When supply lines are short, there is less room for doubt about ethics, about labor practices, and about environmental impacts. The farmer at a local tailgate market will be happy to tell you how she grows her corn. A plate thrown by a local potter is likely to be prettier, and bound to be more unique, than pop-outs from Mikasa. He'll probably even let you watch him throw. Nonlocal products such as gasoline, electronic gizmos or nails can be bought from locally owned businesses instead of megastores, to keep at least some portion of your energy within the local circuit. Better still are co-ops or barter systems that focus benefits in a neighborhood or region.

The bottom line is not, and has never been, price. In the end, what matters is the air we breathe, the food we eat, and the meaning we find in our work and in our lives.

So remember: Buy Here Now.

Jobs? Or work?

If there is a mantra common to all our political gurus, of whatever stripe, it is "Jobs!"

In Congress, at press conferences, at union meetings, in the statehouse and the White House, politicos chant: "Jobs. Jobs. Jobs."

The idea seems to be that people are hungry for jobs. That the government is expected to deliver jobs. That a healthy economy will create jobs. That whatever gods are still held sacred have decreed that jobs are the true goal of a righteous and reverent populace.

Then, why do people so often hate their jobs?

Well, how about this: A whole slew of folks endure their jobs only as a way to convey money from the employer's coffers to theirs. The reason the worker works has nothing to do with family, the community, deep meaning or joy. Instead, the whole enterprise is hung on the hook of bread winning. A job is a cog in the meshing of great economic gears. It links the company bank to the mortgage bank and the auto-loan bank and the supermarket's bank and the oil-company banks and electric-company banks that keep things rolling (cooking, heating, cooling, freezing, telecommunicating and humming) along.

But why, exactly, should it be politically popular to pray, rant, chant or make promises about jobs? Isn't a "job" about as bad as it gets?

We work for things that matter; we take jobs when all else fails. Work is about living, about doing what needs to be done. In our gatherer/hunter past, our work was immediate and tangible. If we gathered, we ate. As agriculture took root, we worked to ensure a continuity of food. We worked to make shelter, or to fashion clothes. There was a direct connection between labor and benefit. There was meaning in what we did when we were intimately linked to cause and effect.

The Job Promise offered by many politicians is completely unhinged from the real world. The scheme is to attract a big employer into a region with tax credits, environmental waivers and other enticements, and the payoff is supposed to be jobs and a boost to the local economy. Nowhere in this equation do we see numbers representing local needs, local history or the local biosphere. The potential cash infusion is presumed to be good—the highest good, beyond question or doubt.

But what about work?

There's a world of difference between hauling wood and shingles, pounding nails and sweating in the summer sun, to put a roof over our heads—and punching in at a plastics factory, a cannery or a software-development facility five days a week, to pay the bills. This is not to demean the labor of those working in industry, but simply to highlight the difference in meaning. Work is done for love; a job is done for money. Work has inherent meaning; a job can easily be meaningless.

Is it a valid function of government to create or attract jobs? Or should the role of the state be to discover what work needs to be done, and find ways for people to do that necessary work—and earn a living wage doing it? Should a government grant hundreds of millions of dollars in tax breaks and incentive programs to a large corporation to induce it to relocate in an economically depressed area? Or should it discover local needs and desires and direct funds toward those ends? The corporate-enticement game automatically assumes the primacy of the global economy over place, life and community. It turns an impoverished local area into a colony to be exploited by foreign powers—who will extract local resources with undervalued labor, in order to enrich unseen barons and brokers. It often permits expanded deforestation and atmospheric or aquatic discharge; subsidizes road, sewer and power infrastructure; and displaces small businesses and residents in the development zone.

Seen in this light, "Jobs!" is not a promise to the people, but a smoke screen. The lofty-sounding, putative goal blurs our view of politicians diverting funds, tax relief and benefits to their corporate backers.

That sounds like a snow job to me.

Dick's and Jane's addictions

Americans spend an average of $350 per child on toys each Christmas. By the time a tyke enters first grade, she's burdened with more than $2,000 worth of plastic trinkets. That adds up to more than $6,000 before high-school graduation—not including birthdays. No wonder folks are building ever-bigger homes: The kids need closet space.

Investing even the first season's toy money might yield a couple thousand bucks over the course of those eighteen Wonder Years; if all the dough were banked, each smiling graduate would be able to afford community college, a decent car, and a weekend in Daytona. But, of course, Americans are notoriously disinclined to save, and if a middle-class kid badly wants college, cars and parties, he will generally figure something out.

No, what concerns me most about this toy story is the lesson we are constantly teaching about "stuff." My grandmother called it "too much of a muchness," and I'm certain Gram was right. We are burying children in mountains of worthless objects, and imbuing them with the idea that possessions have intrinsic worth.

Not one Barbie, but dozens. Not one toy truck, but a fleet. Not a story book, but a multimedia theme park in a box, with voices and beeps and whistles and a corporate mouse logo (software and batteries not included).

Is it any wonder some kids become genuinely aggressive consumers—knifing each other over sneakers and jackets? And mightn't this lead, helter-skelter, to drug use—in which consumption itself becomes the object? A thirst that cannot be quenched results in the ingestion of a whole range of things that are not food. Name your poison, folks: crack, booze, nicotine, chocolate, Prozac, Pepsi, acid, Valium, lithium, heroin, hemlock, Haldol, glue, Coke, coke, uppers, downers and a little of that stuff that slides you sideways. Take two of these, and call me in the morning.

And that's not to mention the present epidemic of eating disorders.

So much muchness, I suspect, also precipitates the healing experience that so many folks discover in nature. When you hike into a wood, up a trail to a mountain summit, or down along a lake, you experience completeness. A tree doesn't need any finishing touches. A quiet pond contains a million million lives, traveling around complete circles of existence. You breathe deeply and relax. Everything is done.

The next time you're tempted to buy a child a lump of painted plastic from Southeast Asia, why not stop in the parking lot, instead? Study the weeds sprouting through the cracks in the asphalt. Follow the line of ants from a spilled soda pop to the anthill over near the curb. Notice the wildflowers blooming among the weeds in the drainage ditch, and the sparrows collecting twigs for building nests in department-store eaves. If you're still drawn inexorably through the welcoming doors, buy a field guide to mammals or birds, instead of a plastic mouse. Your eight-year-old won't understand much except the pictures, but that's why you'll be there—as a teacher and fellow student. Even urban areas are full of wildlife—there are more possums than people in Portland, and foxes are roving in New York's Central Park.

When you teach a child that we are part of the natural world—that humans evolved as part of the great wheel, embedded in the circle of the seasons and the cycle of life and death—you are teaching wholeness. For thirty-five thousand generations, our species lived in harmony with nature. It is only in the past few hundred that we have declared agricultural war on our environment, and only six or ten generations have passed since we began to think we were somehow independent of the rest of creation.

If we have any hope of creating a genuinely sustainable future, it will come only from a deep understanding of our place in the circle of life. And if there is any chance, on a personal level, to escape the false gods of consumerism and economic growth—or their corollary, addiction—it lies in a self-image of completeness and content.

As the adage goes: "Give a child a plastic fish, and entertain her for a day. Teach a child the role of fishes in the biosphere, and you will feed her imagination for a lifetime."

Gorillas in the myth

When a group of folks bands together based on shared beliefs, we usually call it religion—that is, if we credit them with rational suppositions. But if they worship kumquats and believe that tapping their noses with crowbars elevates them toward the divine, we say they embrace myths. Kumquats and crowbars are too much for our scientific, Cartesian logic to allow. No, give us parting seas, angels dancing on the head of a pin, speaking in tongues—or, at least, an ancient turning-wheel-of-life tradition rife with yins and yangs and a fat godhead who contemplates his tummy.

Have you ever noticed that even politicians purportedly at opposite ends of the political spectrum seem to share the same beliefs about economic growth? Did you ever stop to wonder if they all might be *mything* something? When Senator Pete Domenici called Ronald Reagan's pro-growth economic policies "voodoo" the Gipper got so mad he threw a phone against the wall. Of course the Democratic Senator from New Mexico still labors endlessly to grow his home state's economy by diverting massive infusions of Federal cash to the moribund nuclear energy industry.

When politicians tout the benefits of growth, it is almost invariably offered in support of policies good for businesses. Good, that is, in the sense of offering freebees to be paid for by the rest of us.

Adam Smith, the great guru of market theory, pointed out that, in order for market forces to act in everyone's best interests, the producers of goods have to bear all the costs of production. That means that costs have to be internalized. When costs are externalized—that is, paid by someone who doesn't stand to gain or lose from the sale of the product—the market becomes skewed, and it works against society's best interests.

In recent years national, state and local governments are climbing all over each other to lure businesses by promising to externalize their costs. Governors, legislators, even whole city councils, head off on junkets to offer frankincense and myrrh to corporate giants around the globe. "More jobs!" they chant. "Increase the tax base," they sing. "Kumquats! Crowbars! Hallelujah!"

So South Carolinians will pay $130 million over the next 30 years, for the pleasure of having BMW in their neighborhood. And, if the Willamette Chip Mill sneaks into Rutherford County, North Carolinians will ante up nearly a million bucks to improve a couple of roads. Over and over, we are told that it's in our best interest to provide water or sewer hookups, roads, loans, bonds, retraining for prospective workers, or other benefits—to improve the business climate. Gotta get those factories! "Kumquats! Crowbars!"

But companies pay property taxes too, don't they? Aren't they going to help fund all those expensive baubles we're dangling in their faces? Well, actually, no.

Nationwide, corporations paid 43 percent of the nation's property taxes in 1957; today, their share's about 18 percent, and shrinking. One of the first concessions a big outfit demands is reduction of taxes or tax valuation. If that sounds Mickey Mouse—I mean, can't local pols see through a scam that transparent?—it is. When Disney did its World thing in Florida, their real estate was taken off the books. So Floridians pay for infrastructure to provide Goofy with visitors. How thoughtful.

When a candidate tells you that your region should be friendly to business, suggest that it should be friendly to you, instead. Small businesses owned by your friends and neighbors, sole proprietorships, companies with a commitment to the community and a track record of hiring and keeping employees—all these strengthen the social fabric. But, like the standup comedian's gorilla, once you have a transnational corporation in your living room, it can do whatever it wants to.

As a case in point, consider Moore County, S.C. Back in the '70s, they attracted Proctor-Silex with tax breaks, cheap labor and environmental flim-flam. They even tossed in a $5.5 million water-and-sewer bond issue when the plant expanded. But in 1990, Proctor-Silex flew south (because Mexico upped the externalization ante, on all counts)—dumping eight hundred workers. ("More jobs!") Moore County still pays for the bonds and the drums of toxic waste the company forgot to put in its luggage. ("Increase the tax base!")

"Kumquats! Crowbars! Hallelujah!"

Acknowledgements

Who can trace the threads in a tapestry? Or even in the rag rug of my maundering mind? Here are a few to whom I owe particular thanks:

Susan Kay Minor – who was my companion for close to twenty-five years until her untimely death in 2003. For better and for worse, I learned a lot from that relationship.

Peter Gregutt—who edited these pieces for their initial publication inbook form.

David LaMotte—for warm generosity, both material and spiritual, and reminding me to follow my heart. In the time since first publication of this collection, our friendship and my esteem for him have only deepened.

Emoke B'Racz, Bob Falls, Keith Flynn, Bonnie and David Hobbs, Lee Lancaster, and Allan and Ginger Wolf - who together and disparately enabled a city to find its voice.

Greg Olson for *Mountain Voices*, and George Scheibner, who opened the door to public radio and reel-to-reeled me in.

Above all I must thank my readers, particularly those who bite back—feedback loops inexorably generate evolution from chaos.

Each of these individuals is deeply culpable and must accept enduring blame for giving me encouragement. However—pending discovery of a plausible scapegoat—any errors of fact, oddities of opinion, steppings-on-of-toes, woundings of pride, slander, libel, bad advice or painful puns offered herein must be laid at my feet. So be it.

-Cecil Bothwell
January, 2008

About the author

Cecil Bothwell is an investigative reporter based in Asheville, North Carolina. He has received national awards from the Association of Alternative Newsweeklies and the Society of Professional Journalists for investigative reporting, criticism and humorous commentary. He is news editor of *Asheville City Paper*, former managing editor of Asheville's *Mountain Xpress* and founding editor of the Warren Wilson College environmental journal *Heartstone*, he served for several years as a member of the national editorial board of the Association of Alternative Newsweeklies and currently serves on the boards of two international educational nonprofit organizations working in Latin America. His weekly radio and print journal, *Duck Soup: Essays on the Submerging Culture*, remained in syndication for ten years and he currently hosts "Blows Against the Empire," a weekly music and opinion program on WPVM 103.5FM, Asheville (WPVM.org). He blogs at:

http://bothwellsblog.wordpress.com